Wonders

Reading/Writing Companion

Mc
Graw
Hill

mheducation.com/prek-12

Send all inquiries to:
McGraw Hill
1325 Avenue of the Americas
New York, NY 10019

ISBN: 978-1-26-575693-2
MHID: 1-26-575693-7

Printed in the United States of America.

4 5 6 7 8 9 LMN 26 25 24 23 22   A

Welcome to
WONDERS!

We're here to help you set goals to build on the amazing things you already know. We'll also help you reflect on everything you'll learn.

Let's start by taking a look at the incredible things you'll do this year.

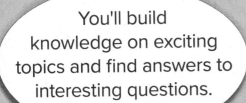

You'll build knowledge on exciting topics and find answers to interesting questions.

You'll read fascinating fiction, informational texts, and poetry and respond to what you read with your own thoughts and ideas.

And you'll research and write stories, poems, and essays of your own!

Here's a sneak peek at how you'll do it all.

"Let's go!"

You'll explore new ideas by reading groups of different texts about the same topic. These groups of texts are called *text sets*.

At the beginning of a text set, we'll help you set goals on the My Goals page. You'll see a bar with four boxes beneath each goal. Think about what you already know to fill in the bar. Here's an example.

I can read and understand narrative nonfiction.

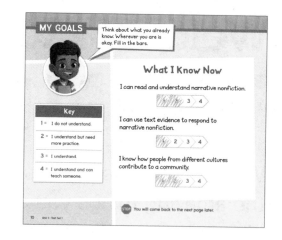

As you move through a text set, you'll explore an essential question and build your knowledge of a topic until you're ready to write about it yourself.

You'll also learn skills that will help you reach your text set goals. At the end of lessons, you'll see a new Check In bar with four boxes.

CHECK IN 1 2 3 4

Reflect on how well you understood a lesson to fill in the bar.

Here are some questions you can ask yourself.

- Was I able to complete the task?

- Was it easy, or was it hard?

- Do I think I need more practice?

You have plenty of tools and resources to learn more, such as anchor charts and center activities. You can also reread a lesson or ask a teacher or peer for help.

It's okay if I think I need more practice. The most important thing is that I do my best and keep learning!

Thinking about what works best for me will help me choose what to do next.

At the end of each text set, you'll show off the knowledge you built by completing a fun task. Then you'll return to the second My Goals page where we'll help you reflect on all that you learned.

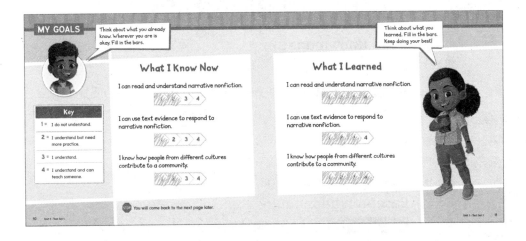

TEXT SET 1 **BIOGRAPHY**

TEXT SET 2 **FAIRY TALE**

Emmett Loverde/Moment Open/Getty Images

TEXT SET 3 **ARGUMENTATIVE TEXT**

EXTENDED WRITING

CONNECT AND REFLECT

 Digital Tools

Find this eBook and other resources at **my.mheducation.com**

TEXT SET 1 **BIOGRAPHY**

TEXT SET 2 **DRAMA/MYTH**

Time Life Pictures/NASA/The LIFE Picture Collection/Getty Images

TEXT SET 3 **POETRY**

EXTENDED WRITING

CONNECT AND REFLECT

Digital Tools

Find this eBook and other resources at **my.mheducation.com**

Build Knowledge

Essential Question

What do good citizens do?

Build Vocabulary

Write new words you learned about citizens and what good citizens do. Draw lines and circles for the words you write.

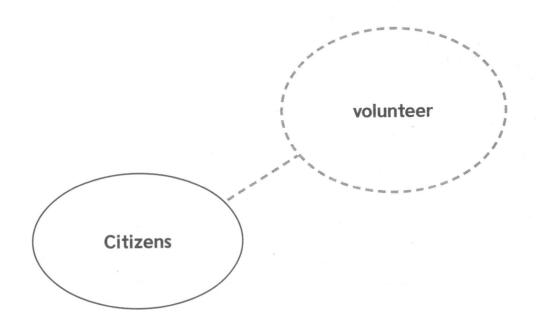

volunteer

Citizens

Go online to **my.mheducation.com** and read the Blast titled "The Generous Grower." Think about why it's important to learn about good citizens. Then blast back your response.

Emmett Loverde/Moment Open/Getty Images

Think about what you already know. Fill in the bars. You'll learn more with practice.

What I Know Now

I can read and understand a biography.

| 1 | 2 | 3 | 4 |

Key
1 = I do not understand.
2 = I understand but need more practice.
3 = I understand.
4 = I understand and can teach someone.

I can use text evidence to respond to a biography.

| 1 | 2 | 3 | 4 |

I know what good citizens do.

| 1 | 2 | 3 | 4 |

STOP You will come back to the next page later.

Think about what you learned. Fill in the bars. What is getting easier for you?

What I Learned

I can read and understand a biography.

1 > 2 > 3 > 4

I can use text evidence to respond to a biography.

1 > 2 > 3 > 4

I know what good citizens do.

1 > 2 > 3 > 4

My Goal I can read and understand a biography.

TAKE NOTES

As you read, make note of interesting words and important information.

_____

_____

_____

_____

_____

_____

_____

_____

_____

_____

Dolores Huerta
GROWING UP STRONG

Essential Question

What do good citizens do?

Read how Dolores Huerta's actions helped many people.

Arthur Schatz/The LIFE Picture Collection/Getty Images

Dolores Huerta learned to help people by watching her mother. Good **citizenship** was important to her, and she taught Dolores that women can be strong leaders. When Dolores grew up, she had the same beliefs.

Good Citizens

Dolores was born on April 10, 1930. She lived in a small town in New Mexico until she was three years old. Then she moved to California with her mother and two brothers. Dolores grew up watching her mother **participate** in community organizations. Her mother believed that all people deserve to be treated fairly.

When Dolores was a young girl, her mother owned a hotel and a restaurant. Many farm workers who lived in their town were poor and hungry. They were paid very little for their hard work. Dolores's mother let them stay at her hotel and eat at her restaurant for free. This taught Dolores and her brothers that good citizens get involved in the community by helping their neighbors.

Dolores Huerta helped farm workers who spent many hours working in fields.

Dr. Parvinder Sethi

BIOGRAPHY

FIND TEXT EVIDENCE

Read

Paragraph 1
Ask and Answer Questions
What two things did Dolores learn from her mother? **Circle** text evidence to answer.

Paragraphs 2–3
Author's Claim
What does the author think of Dolores's mother?

_____

_____

Underline details the author gives that support this claim.

Captions
Draw a box around something new you learned in the caption.

Reread
Author's Craft
Why is "Good Citizens" a good heading for this section?

FIND TEXT EVIDENCE 🔍

Read

Paragraphs 1–2

Ask and Answer Questions

Ask yourself a question about Dolores's students. Write it here.

_____

_____

Draw a box around the answer.

Paragraph 3

Author's Claim

Underline details that show what the author thinks about how Dolores helped her students.

Timelines

Look at the timeline. What year did Dolores meet Cesar Chavez?

_____

Reread

Author's Craft

How does the author help you understand what life was like for Dolores's students?

Dolores Goes to School

Dolores saw how hard life was for farm workers in California. She wanted everyone to be treated fairly. This attitude **continued** as she attended college and studied to become a teacher.

Many of the students that Dolores taught were the children of farm workers. These students were often tired and hungry. They came to school barefoot because they had no shoes. Dolores knew she needed to help them. As a result, she went to her school's principal and **proposed** some good ideas. She tried to get free lunches and milk for the children. She tried to get them new clothes and shoes.

Trying to help the children was a **daring** thing for Dolores to do. The other teachers did not agree with her ideas. Dolores risked a lot, but her beliefs did not **waver**. She decided to do something about the **unfairness** she saw. She wanted to find a better way to help farm workers and their families.

Dolores: Strong and Fair

This is a timeline. It shows important dates in Dolores Huerta's life.

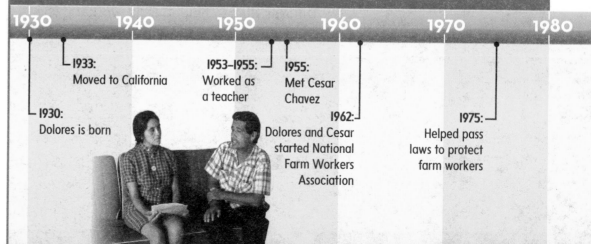

| 1930 | 1940 | 1950 | 1960 | 1970 | 1980 |

1933: Moved to California

1930: Dolores is born

1953–1955: Worked as a teacher

1955: Met Cesar Chavez

1962: Dolores and Cesar started National Farm Workers Association

1975: Helped pass laws to protect farm workers

Arthur Schatz/The LIFE Picture Collection/Getty Images

Dolores Stands Strong

Every day Dolores saw people working in unusually unsafe and disagreeable conditions. She was **horrified**. Many farm workers had little money to feed their families. Dolores decided to do something.

In 1955, Dolores met Cesar Chavez. He wanted to make life better for farm workers, too. Dolores and Cesar organized the workers into a group called the National Farm Workers Association. This group protected the rights of the farm workers. It helped make big farms treat them better. As a result, working conditions on the farms improved.

Growing up with a mother who cared about other people taught Dolores to be a good citizen. Her kind and brave acts helped farm workers and their families. Who is a good citizen? Dolores Huerta is!

Dolores Huerta speaks for farm workers at a rally in 1969.

(t)1976 George Ballis/Take Stock/The Image Works, (b)J. Scott Applewhite/AP Images

1990   2000   2010

1998: Earned Human Rights Award from President Clinton

Summarize

Review your notes and think about what you learned from "Dolores Huerta: Growing Up Strong." Summarize the text using the central idea and relevant details.

FIND TEXT EVIDENCE

Read

Paragraph 1

Prefixes and Suffixes

Circle the base word in *disagreeable*. Use the prefix and suffix to write what *disagreeable* means.

_____

_____

Paragraphs 2–3

Ask and Answer Questions

How did Dolores and Cesar help the farm workers?

_____

_____

_____

Underline text evidence.

Reread

Author's Craft

How does the author show that Dolores is strong?

Vocabulary

Use the sentences to talk with a partner about each word. Then answer the questions.

citizenship

Planting a tree in your community is an example of good **citizenship**.

What can you do to show good citizenship in your community?

_____

_____

continued

Luis **continued** to read his book all afternoon.

What is the opposite of *continued*?

_____

_____

daring

It is **daring** to stand up for your beliefs.

Write about something daring you have done.

_____

_____

horrified

Pam was **horrified** when she saw what the storm did to the bird's nest.

What does it mean to feel horrified?

_____

_____

participate

Neena's friends like to **participate** in sports.

What games do you like to participate in?

_____

_____

Build Your Word List Draw a box around the word *conditions* in the first paragraph on page 15. Look up the word's meaning using a classroom or online dictionary. In your reader's notebook, write down the word and its definition.

proposed

Dad **proposed** they look online to find the answer to Kia's question.

Write about something you proposed to your family or friends.

_____

_____

unfairness

Our coach discussed the **unfairness** of the referee's decision.

What word means the opposite of _unfairness?_

_____

_____

waver

Ted's confidence started to **waver** when he forgot the answer.

Describe how you would look if your confidence started to waver.

_____

_____

Prefixes and Suffixes

A prefix is a word part added to the beginning of a word. A suffix is added to the end of a word. To figure out the meaning of a word with a prefix and suffix, find the base word first.

🔍 FIND TEXT EVIDENCE

I see the word unfairness _on page 14. I find the base word_ fair _first. I know the prefix_ un- _means "not." The suffix_ -ness _means "state or condition of." Unfairness_ means "the state of not being fair."

> She decided to do something about the unfairness she saw.

Your Turn Find the base word in the word below. Then use the prefix and suffix to figure out the word's meaning.

unusually, page 15 _____

_____

CHECK IN ⟩ 1 ⟩ 2 ⟩ 3 ⟩ 4 ⟩

Dr. Parvinder Sethi

Ask and Answer Questions

Ask yourself questions as you read. Then read on or reread to find the answers.

🔍 FIND TEXT EVIDENCE

Look at the section "Good Citizens" on page 13. Think of a question and then reread to find the answer.

Quick Tip

Look for signal words to help you answer your questions. For example, words and phrases such as *then*, *next*, and *before* can help you understand the order of events.

Page 13

Good Citizens

Dolores was born on April 10, 1930. She lived in a small town in New Mexico until she was three years old. Then she moved to California with her mother and two brothers. Dolores grew up watching her mother **participate** in community organizations. Her mother believed that all people deserve to be treated fairly.

When Dolores was a young girl, her mother owned a hotel and a restaurant. Many farm workers who lived in their town were poor and hungry. They were paid very little for their hard work. Dolores's mother let them stay at her hotel and eat at her restaurant for free. This taught Dolores and her brothers that good citizens get involved in the community by helping their neighbors.

I have a question. How did Dolores learn to be a good citizen? I read that <u>when Dolores was young, her mother let farm workers eat and live for free at her hotel.</u> Now I can answer my question. Dolores learned to be a good citizen by watching her mother.

Your Turn Reread "Dolores Goes to School" on page 14. Think of a question with a partner. You might ask how Dolores tried to help the children in her class. Reread to find the answer and write it below.

_____

_____

CHECK IN ⟩ 1 ⟩ 2 ⟩ 3 ⟩ 4 ⟩

Captions and Timelines

"Dolores Huerta: Growing Up Strong" is a **biography**. A biography

- is written by an author to inform readers about the true story of a real person's life
- includes text features, such as timelines, photographs, and captions, to support the author's purpose

FIND TEXT EVIDENCE

I can tell that "Dolores Huerta: Growing Up Strong" is a biography. The author's purpose is to give facts and information about Dolores Huerta's life. There are many text features, such as a timeline that shows important events in Dolores Huerta's life.

Readers to Writers

Text features contribute, or add, meaning to a text in different ways. A timeline, for example, can help readers understand the order of dates and events that are mentioned in a text. Think about how you can use a timeline in your own writing.

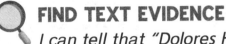

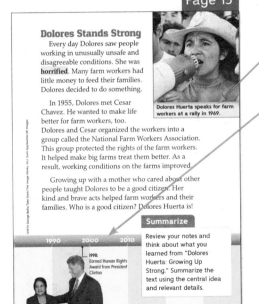

Page 15

Dolores Stands Strong

Every day Dolores saw people working in unusually unsafe and disagreeable conditions. She was **horrified**. Many farm workers had little money to feed their families. Dolores decided to do something.

In 1955, Dolores met Cesar Chavez. He wanted to make life better for farm workers, too. Dolores and Cesar organized the workers into a group called the National Farm Workers Association. This group protected the rights of the farm workers. It helped make big farms treat them better. As a result, working conditions on the farms improved.

Growing up with a mother who cared about other people taught Dolores to be a good citizen. Her kind and brave acts helped farm workers and their families. Who is a good citizen? Dolores Huerta is!

Dolores Huerta speaks for farm workers at a rally in 1969.

1990   2000   2010

1998: Earned Human Rights Award from President Clinton

Summarize

Review your notes and think about what you learned from "Dolores Huerta: Growing Up Strong." Summarize the text using the central idea and relevant details.

Captions

A caption describes what is happening in a photograph. It gives information that is not included in the main text.

Timelines

A timeline shows the order of important events and the dates on which they happened.

Your Turn Look at the timeline on pages 14 and 15. When did Dolores and Cesar start the National Farm Workers Association?

COLLABORATE

CHECK IN 1 2 3 4

Author's Claim

An author's claim is something the author believes to be true. Strong claims are supported by evidence, such as facts and examples. To find an author's claim, look for details that reveal the author's thoughts and feelings. Then think about what the details have in common.

 FIND TEXT EVIDENCE

What does the author think about Dolores Huerta? I can reread and look for details that tell me what the author thinks. This will help me figure out the author's claim.

Details
Dolores's mother taught her that good citizens get involved in their communities.
Helping her students was a daring thing for Dolores to do.

Author's Claim

 Your Turn Reread "Dolores Huerta: Growing Up Strong." Find another detail that tells how the author feels about Dolores. Add it to your graphic organizer. Then see what the details have in common to figure out the author's claim about Dolores Huerta.

CHECK IN 1 > 2 > 3 > 4 >

Details
Dolores's mother taught her that good citizens get involved in their communities.
Helping her students was a daring thing for Dolores to do.

Author's Claim

Respond to Reading

COLLABORATE Talk about the prompt below. Use your notes and evidence from the text to support your answer.

How is Dolores Huerta a good citizen?

_____

_____

_____

_____

_____

_____

_____

_____

Quick Tip

You can use these sentence starters to talk about the prompt.

Dolores Huerta is a good citizen because . . .

One example of Dolores Huerta's good citizenship is . . .

Grammar Connections

As you write your response, be sure to capitalize the names of people and organizations. Remember to use the correct punctuation at the end of each sentence.

CHECK IN 1 2 3 4

Volunteers in Your Community

Every community has people and groups who volunteer their time to solve problems. Work with a partner to choose a group that works to solve a problem in your community. Follow the research process to learn more about what the group does. Then create a poster to show what you learned.

Step 1 **Set a Goal** Choose a group working to solve an issue in your local community.

Step 2 **Identify Sources** Think of questions to answer through research. You could ask what your group does to help, or when and where the group began. Find primary and secondary sources that can answer your questions. Primary sources are by people who experience something firsthand. Secondary sources are by people who did not experience something for themselves.

Step 3 **Find and Record Information** Record information from your sources that answers your questions. Remember to cite your sources.

Step 4 **Organize and Combine Information** Start to think about your poster. What information will you include? What photos or illustrations could you add?

Step 5 **Create and Present** Create your final poster with your partner. Share your work with the class. Tell where you found your information.

> **Quick Tip**
>
> Volunteer organizations in your community might clean up litter from parks and rivers, organize food drives and book drives, help the elderly, or register people to vote.

Clean Up Our Park

Royal Freedman/Alamy Stock Photo

CHECK IN 1 2 3 4

Elizabeth Leads the Way:
Elizabeth Cady Stanton and the Right to Vote

Literature Anthology:
pages 366–383

 How does the author use what Elizabeth says and does to help you understand her personality?

 Talk About It Reread **Literature Anthology** pages 370 and 371. Discuss with a partner what Elizabeth Cady Stanton says and does.

Cite Text Evidence What does Elizabeth say and do? In the chart, write text evidence and how it helps you understand Elizabeth.

Text Evidence	What It Tells About Elizabeth

Write The author uses what Elizabeth says and does to help me

understand that _____

_____

Make Inferences

An inference is a conclusion based on facts and evidence. What inference can you make about Elizabeth based on the title *Elizabeth Leads the Way: Elizabeth Cady Stanton and the Right to Vote*?

CHECK IN 1 2 3 4

How do you know that Elizabeth felt strongly about what she believed in?

 Talk About It Reread **Literature Anthology** page 379. Talk with a partner about what Elizabeth thinks about a woman's right to vote.

Cite Text Evidence When you cite text evidence, you look for text that supports your response. What words help you understand how strong Elizabeth's feelings are? Write text evidence in the chart.

Text Evidence	How Elizabeth Felt

Write I know that Elizabeth felt strongly about her beliefs because

the author _____

_____

_____

Quick Tip

You can use these sentence starters to talk about Elizabeth.

I read that Elizabeth . . .

This helps me understand that . . .

 Synthesize Information

Make a personal connection to what you read about Elizabeth Cady Stanton. Perhaps you have felt unfairness, too. When you make a personal connection to a text, you can deepen your understanding of what you have read.

CHECK IN 1 2 3 4

? **How does the author help you understand how Elizabeth's ideas changed America?**

Talk About It Reread **Literature Anthology** pages 382 and 383. Discuss why the author uses the phrase "spread like wildfire."

Cite Text Evidence What other words and phrases show how Elizabeth changed America? Write text evidence in the chart.

Quick Tip

The author uses the phrase "spread like wildfire" to help you picture how quickly Elizabeth's ideas spread.

Text Evidence	What It Means
How It Helps You Understand How Elizabeth Changed America	

Write The author helps me understand how Elizabeth changed

America by _____

_____

CHECK IN 1 2 3 4

My Goal I can use text evidence to respond to a biography.

Respond to Reading

COLLABORATE Talk about the prompt below. Use your notes and evidence from the text to support your answer.

How did Elizabeth Cady Stanton show good citizenship?

_____

_____

_____

_____

_____

_____

_____

_____

_____

_____

Quick Tip

You can use these sentence starters to talk about the prompt.

Elizabeth Cady Stanton showed good citizenship by . . .

One thing Elizabeth Cady Stanton did was . . .

CHECK IN 1 2 3 4

Susan B. Anthony Takes Action!

Literature Anthology: pages 386–389

1.   Susan Brownell Anthony was born in Massachusetts in 1820. Her family believed that all people are equal. At the time Susan was born, however, this idea of equality was very unusual. Men and women did not have the same rights. Women could not vote and they could not own property. Life was different for Susan. She learned to read and write at the age of three, even though she was a girl.

Reread and use the prompts to take notes in the text.

Circle words and phrases that help you understand what equality is. Write what equality means on the lines below.

_____

_____

_____

_____

COLLABORATE

Talk with a partner about how life was different for Susan. **Underline** text evidence in the excerpt that supports what you said.

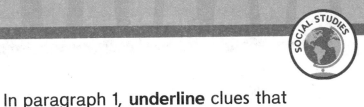

Women Get the Vote!

1   Susan gave as many as 100 speeches around the country every year for forty-five years. She always stayed excited and hopeful about her work.

2   Not everyone agreed with her ideas. Susan and her friend Elizabeth Cady Stanton had to fight hard for many years for the rights of all people. They always did their work peacefully. It was not until fourteen years after Susan died that women in the United States were allowed to vote. The long struggle would not have been successful without the work of Susan B. Anthony.

In paragraph 1, **underline** clues that help you visualize what Susan was like. Summarize them on the lines below.

_____

_____

_____

_____

_____

_____

COLLABORATE

Reread paragraph 2. Talk with a partner about how other people felt about Susan's ideas. What did Susan and Elizabeth do? **Circle** words and phrases that show what they did. **Make a check mark** before the sentence that shows how the author feels about Susan.

How does the author help you know how she feels about Susan B. Anthony?

 Talk About It Reread paragraph 2 on page 29. Talk about what the author says about Susan.

Cite Text Evidence What words let you know how the author feels about Susan and the work she did? Write text evidence in the chart.

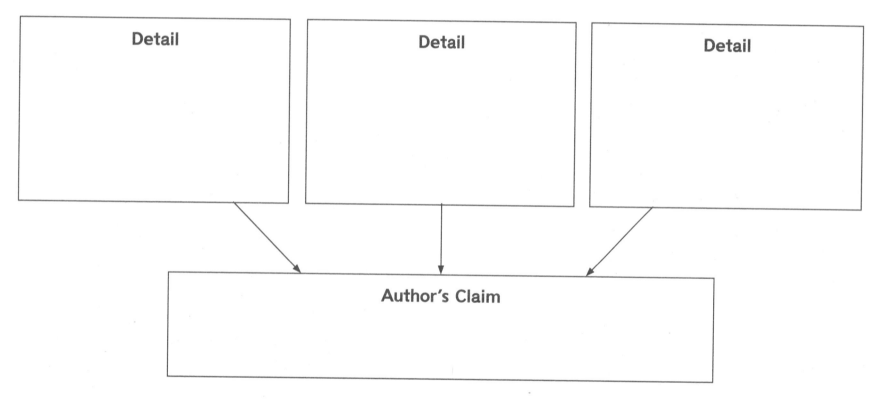

Detail	Detail	Detail

Author's Claim

Write The author lets me know how she feels about Susan B. Anthony by

_____

_____

CHECK IN 1 2 3 4

Cause and Effect

One way for an author to structure a text is by using cause and effect. An effect is something that happened. A cause is why it happened. By telling why an event happened or what happened because of it, authors can help readers better understand a topic.

Readers to Writers

Use signal words to help your readers figure out cause and effect. Some signal words and phrases are *because, so, therefore,* and *as a result.*

FIND TEXT EVIDENCE

On page 387 of "Susan B. Anthony Takes Action!" in the **Literature Anthology**, the author uses the phrase *as a result* to show what happened when Susan's teacher refused to teach her long division.

As a result, Susan's family took her out of school and taught her at home.

Your Turn Reread the last paragraph on page 387 with a partner. Use text evidence to answer the questions below.

• How do you know what caused Susan to work with Elizabeth?

_____

_____

• How do the author's words help you see how Susan felt about

Elizabeth's work? _____

_____

CHECK IN 1 2 3 4

MAKE CONNECTIONS

? **How do the lyrics of "America" and the people you read about in *Elizabeth Leads the Way* and "Susan B. Anthony Takes Action!" show you what good citizens do?**

Talk About It Read the song lyrics. Talk with a partner about how the speaker feels about America.

Cite Text Evidence **Underline** words and phrases in the lyrics that show what the speaker values about America.

Write The lyrics of "America" and the selections I read help me understand what good citizens do because

_____

_____

_____

_____

_____

_____

_____

AMERICA

My country 'tis of thee,
Sweet land of liberty,
Of thee I sing.
Land where my fathers died,
Land of the Pilgrim's pride,
From ev'ry mountainside
Let freedom ring.

—Lyrics by Samuel F. Smith

Smith, Samuel F. "America." 1831

SHOW YOUR KNOWLEDGE

Write a Recipe

Think over what you learned about what good citizens do. How do people's good deeds and actions improve their communities and the world?

1. Look at your Build Knowledge notes in your reader's notebook.

2. Brainstorm a list of qualities that make someone a good citizen. Some examples of qualities are bravery, honesty, and kindness. Think about the people you read about to help you make your list.

3. Use your list of qualities to write a recipe for a good citizen. Write step-by-step instructions that explain which qualities you would add together to create a good citizen.

4. Add a sentence that explains why it is important to be a good citizen and how it can make your community better. Use new vocabulary words you have learned.

Think about what you learned in this text set. Fill in the bars on page 11.

Build Knowledge

? **Essential Question**

How do we get what we need?

Build Vocabulary

Write new words you learned about trade and how we get what we need. Draw lines and circles for the words you write.

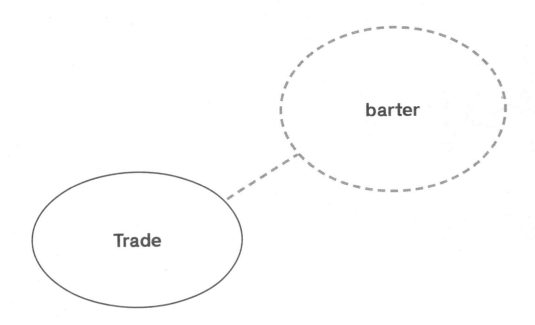

barter

Trade

Go online to **my.mheducation.com** and read the "Strictly Business" Blast. Think about why it's important to know how businesses get what they need. Then blast back your response.

Think about what you already know. Fill in the bars. Keep doing your best!

What I Know Now

I can read and understand a fairy tale.

1 > 2 > 3 > 4 >

I can use text evidence to respond to a fairy tale.

1 > 2 > 3 > 4 >

I know how we get what we need.

1 > 2 > 3 > 4 >

Key	
1 =	I do not understand.
2 =	I understand but need more practice.
3 =	I understand.
4 =	I understand and can teach someone.

 You will come back to the next page later.

Think about what you learned. Fill in the bars. You can always improve, so keep trying!

What I Learned

I can read and understand a fairy tale.

1 > 2 > 3 > 4

I can use text evidence to respond to a fairy tale.

1 > 2 > 3 > 4

I know how we get what we need.

1 > 2 > 3 > 4

My Goal I can read and understand a fairy tale.

TAKE NOTES

As you read, make note of interesting words and important events.

Juanita and the Beanstalk

Essential Question

How do we get what we need?

Read about what Juanita does to get what she needs.

Juanita lived in a small, **humble** cottage with her Mamá and her pet goat, Pepe.

One day Mamá said, "There has been no rain, and our garden has dried up. Juanita, you must go to town and sell your goat. Use the money you get as **payment** to buy some food."

"I don't want to sell Pepe!" cried Juanita. She petted the goat lovingly. But she was an obedient girl and would not disobey her mother. **Reluctantly**, she took Pepe to town. On her way she met an old man who patted Pepe kindly.

"He is for sale," said Juanita with tears in her eyes.

The man replied, "I have no money, but I have some special *frijoles*. If you plant these beans, you will never go hungry again. We can **barter**, and I will trade you these beans for your goat."

FIND TEXT EVIDENCE

Read

Paragraphs 1–2

Summarize

What does Mamá tell Juanita to do? **Circle** text evidence.

Paragraphs 3–5

Base Words

Draw a box around *lovingly*. What is its base word?

_____

Character Perspective

How does Juanita feel about her mother's request?

_____

_____

_____

Underline details that tell how Juanita feels.

Reread

Author's Craft

How does the author help you understand what *frijoles* means?

SHARED READ

FIND TEXT EVIDENCE 🔍

Read

Paragraph 1
Theme

Underline text evidence that helps you understand why Juanita accepts the man's offer.

Paragraphs 2–3
Character Perspective

How does Mamá feel about Juanita's decision?

_____

_____

Circle text evidence.

Paragraphs 4–6
Summarize

Why does the maid tell Juanita to hide? **Draw a box around the reason.**

Reread

Author's Craft

How does the author help you visualize the beanstalk?

Juanita thought carefully as she **considered** the man's offer. He seemed caring and considerate. Certainly he would be kind to Pepe, so Juanita finally decided to sell Pepe. She accepted the beans.

When Juanita got home, Mamá was upset with her decision. "You have returned home with no food and no money!" she exclaimed.

Juanita had to **admit** that Mamá was right. All she had were three beans, and she still missed Pepe. Worst of all, Mamá was unhappy.

Juanita planted the beans in the backyard and went to bed. The next morning she woke up and went outside. A gigantic beanstalk as tall as the clouds stood where Juanita had planted the beans.

Juanita was curious. "I'm going to see what's up there," she said to herself, so Juanita climbed the beanstalk. At the top she saw a grand and **magnificent** palace in the middle of a field. She knocked on the door, and a maid answered.

"Hide!" cried the maid. "The giant is coming now, and he doesn't like strangers." So Juanita quickly crawled under the table.

The giant stomped in carrying an unhappy hen in a cage. He said, "Lay, hen, lay!" Juanita's curiosity grew, and she peeked from under the table. Then she saw the hen's **creation**. Juanita gasped. It was a golden egg!

The poor hen reminded Juanita of Pepe. She wanted to give it a better home. She ran between the giant's legs and grabbed the cage. She raced to the beanstalk. The giant roared in anger and chased after her. Juanita was able to slide down the beanstalk, but the giant was too heavy. He caused the stalk to break and crash to the ground. The beanstalk was gone forever, and Juanita and the hen were safe.

The hen was happy to have a new home and laid many golden eggs. Mamá was happy to use the eggs to buy everything they needed. And Juanita was happy because she was able to trade a golden egg with the old man to get Pepe back!

FIND TEXT EVIDENCE

Read

Paragraphs 1–2
Character Perspective
How does Juanita feel about the hen?

_____

_____

Circle text evidence.

Paragraph 3
Theme
How do things end happily for Juanita and Mamá?
Underline text evidence.

_____

_____

Reread
Author's Craft
How does the author help you understand how Juanita feels at the end of the fairy tale?

Summarize

Use your notes and think about what happens in "Juanita and the Beanstalk." Summarize the text using the plot and theme.

Vocabulary

Use the sentences to talk with a partner about each word. Then answer the questions.

admit

María had to **admit** to her mom that she had broken the plate.

What is something you had to admit?

_____

_____

barter

Ashton likes to **barter**, or trade, toys with Kim.

What is another word for *barter*?

_____

_____

considered

Manuel thought carefully as he **considered** which apple to buy.

What is something you considered doing?

_____

_____

creation

Ella admired her **creation** in art class.

What is a creation you have made?

_____

_____

humble

My grandfather's house is **humble**, simple, and plain.

What is the opposite of *humble*?

_____

_____

Build Your Word List Reread the first paragraph on page 41. Draw a box around the word *gasped*. Look up the definition of the word *gasped* using a dictionary. In your reader's notebook, make a list of words that mean almost the same as *gasped*. Use one of them in a sentence.

magnificent

Li took a picture of the **magnificent** sunset.

What is something magnificent you've seen?

_____

_____

payment

Mom gave our neighbor **payment** for the books.

What do people usually use for payment?

_____

_____

reluctantly

The goats stepped **reluctantly** down the steep path.

How would you raise your hand reluctantly?

_____

_____

Base Words

A base word is the simplest form of a word. When you read an unfamiliar word, you can use its base word to figure out what the word means.

🔍 FIND TEXT EVIDENCE

On page 40, I see the word considerate. *I think the base word is* consider. *I know that* consider *means "to think about it." Being considerate must mean "thoughtful of others' feelings."*

Juanita thought carefully as she considered the man's offer. He seemed caring and considerate.

Your Turn Find the base word in each word. Then use it to figure out each word's meaning.

decision, page 40 _____

_____

curiosity, page 41 _____

_____

CHECK IN ▷ 1 ▷ 2 ▷ 3 ▷ 4 ▷

Summarize

When you summarize, you retell the most important events in a story. Use details to help you summarize "Juanita and the Beanstalk."

🔍 FIND TEXT EVIDENCE

Why does Juanita have to sell her pet goat? Identify important story events. Then summarize them in your own words.

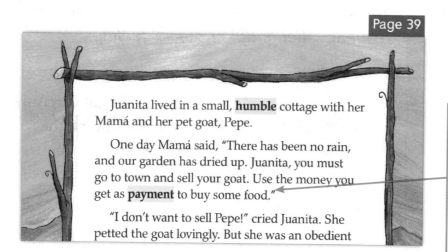

Page 39

Juanita lived in a small, **humble** cottage with her Mamá and her pet goat, Pepe.

One day Mamá said, "There has been no rain, and our garden has dried up. Juanita, you must go to town and sell your goat. Use the money you get as **payment** to buy some food."

"I don't want to sell Pepe!" cried Juanita. She petted the goat lovingly. But she was an obedient

I read that it hadn't rained, and Mamá's garden dried up. They needed money for food. Mamá told Juanita to sell Pepe, her pet goat. These details help me summarize. Juanita had to sell her goat to get money for food.

COLLABORATE

Your Turn Reread "Juanita and the Beanstalk." Summarize the most important events that tell how Juanita found the giant's palace.

_____

_____

_____

CHECK IN 1 ⟩ 2 ⟩ 3 ⟩ 4 ⟩

Theme

"Juanita and the Beanstalk" is a **fairy tale**. A fairy tale

- is a made-up story with events that could not really happen
- often has magical characters or settings and a happy ending
- has a theme, or message, that develops throughout the plot

FIND TEXT EVIDENCE

I can tell that "Juanita and the Beanstalk" is a fairy tale. It has magical characters and events that could not really happen. There's also a happy ending and a theme that develops throughout the plot.

Page 41

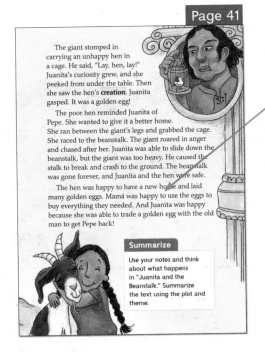

The giant stomped in carrying an unhappy hen in a cage. He said, "Lay, hen, lay!" Juanita's curiosity grew, and she peeked from under the table. Then she saw the hen's **creation**. Juanita gasped. It was a golden egg!

The poor hen reminded Juanita of Pepe. She wanted to give it a better home. She ran between the giant's legs and grabbed the cage. She raced to the beanstalk. The giant roared in anger and chased after her. Juanita was able to slide down the beanstalk, but the giant was too heavy. He caused the stalk to break and crash to the ground. The beanstalk was gone forever, and Juanita and the hen were safe.

The hen was happy to have a new home and laid many golden eggs. Mamá was happy to use the eggs to buy everything they needed. And Juanita was happy because she was able to trade a golden egg with the old man to get Pepe back!

Summarize
Use your notes and think about what happens in "Juanita and the Beanstalk." Summarize the text using the plot and theme.

Theme

The theme is the main message an author wants the reader to remember. Use details, such as plot events or a character's perspective, to see how a theme develops.

COLLABORATE

Your Turn Discuss with a partner what you think could be a theme, or message, in "Juanita and the Beanstalk." Use details from the story to support your answer.

_____

_____

_____

CHECK IN 1 2 3 4

Character Perspective

Characters in fiction often have different perspectives, or thoughts and feelings about other characters, events, or ideas. Details in a story can help you figure out a character's perspective. Pay attention to what characters say, what they think, and how they respond, or react, in different situations.

FIND TEXT EVIDENCE

In the beginning of "Juanita and the Beanstalk," Mamá asks Juanita to sell their pet goat, Pepe. I can reread page 39 to understand how Juanita feels about Pepe. Details that show what Juanita says and does help me understand her perspective.

Details
"I don't want to sell Pepe!" cried Juanita.
She petted the goat lovingly.

↓

Perspective

Your Turn Find more details in the text and illustrations on pages 38 and 39 that show Juanita's feelings about Pepe. Add your details to the graphic organizer, and use them to figure out Juanita's perspective.

CHECK IN 1 2 3 4

Details

↓

Perspective

Respond to Reading

My Goal I can use text evidence to respond to a fairy tale.

COLLABORATE Talk about the prompt below. Use your notes and evidence from the text to support your answer.

How can you tell that Pepe is important to Juanita?

_____

_____

_____

_____

_____

_____

_____

_____

_____

Quick Tip

Use these sentence starters to talk about the prompt.

I know Pepe is important to Juanita because . . .

Juanita thinks Pepe is . . .

Grammar Connections

As you write your response, think about the order of events that affect Juanita's perspective. Use signal words, such as *first, next, then,* and *finally,* to help readers follow the order of events.

CHECK IN 1 2 3 4

Business Plans

Every business needs a plan to get what it needs. The first step is knowing what to sell. Then you list the supplies you need. Next, you decide how to advertise and how much to charge. Finally, you set a goal. Work with a partner and follow the research process to create a plan for a business of your own.

Quick Tip

You need to charge more than you spend. List how much your supplies cost. Think how much people will be willing to pay. Then decide what to charge.

Step 1 **Set a Goal** Brainstorm ideas for a business, such as a dog-walking service or lemonade stand. Choose your favorite idea.

Step 2 **Identify Sources** Think of research questions that will help you with your plan. You should ask about the supplies you'll need, how much you should charge, and how you'll advertise. Find books, reliable websites, or a trusted adult to help you answer your questions.

BUSINESS PLAN

What to sell: _Lemonade_

Supplies: _lemons, water, sugar, pitcher, glasses, stand_

How to advertise: _____

What to Charge: _____

Your goal: _____

Step 3 **Find and Record Information** Take notes on your sources. Remember to cite your sources.

Step 4 **Organize and Combine Information** Sort your notes and identify the most helpful information. Then create a draft of your business plan.

Step 5 **Create and Present** Create your final business plan. Add photos or illustrations before you present your plan to the class. You can use the plan for a lemonade stand as a model.

CHECK IN   1   2   3   4

Clever Jack Takes the Cake

 How does the way the author repeats words and phrases help you understand Jack's character?

Literature Anthology: pages 390–407

Talk About It Reread the fifth paragraph on **Literature Anthology** page 393. Talk with a partner about what Jack is doing.

Cite Text Evidence What words does the author repeat? Write text evidence and explain how it helps you understand what Jack is like.

Text Evidence	What Jack Is Like

Write The author uses repetition to help me understand that Jack is

_____

_____

Make Inferences

Use text evidence and what you know to make an inference. An inference is a conclusion based on facts. What inference can you make about how much time Jack is spending in the strawberry patch?

CHECK IN 1 2 3 4

? **How does the author use language to help you visualize what the bear is doing?**

Talk About It Reread **Literature Anthology** page 401. Talk with your partner about what the bear does.

Cite Text Evidence What words and phrases help you visualize what happens to Jack's cake? Write text evidence in the chart.

Text Evidence	What I Visualize

Write The author uses words and phrases to help me visualize _____

_____

_____

Quick Tip

You can use these sentence starters to talk about the author's word choice.

The author uses words and phrases to . . .

This helps me visualize . . .

 Make Inferences

Use text evidence and what you know to make an inference. What inference can you make about why the bear was dancing around?

CHECK IN 1 ⟩ 2 ⟩ 3 ⟩ 4

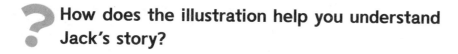
? **How does the illustration help you understand Jack's story?**

COLLABORATE

Talk About It Reread **Literature Anthology** page 404 and look at the illustration. Talk with a partner about the parts of Jack's story.

Cite Text Evidence What clues in the illustration help you understand what Jack tells the princess? Write clues in the chart.

Illustration Clue	What It Helps Me Understand

Write The author uses the illustration to help me see that Jack

_____

_____

Quick Tip

When you reread, you can use illustrations to understand more about the story.

Evaluate Information

Jack gulps and shuffles his feet before greeting the princess. What does this say about how Jack is feeling?

CHECK IN 1 2 3 4

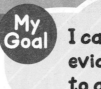
Respond to Reading

COLLABORATE
Talk about the prompt below. Use your notes and evidence from the text to support your answer.

Do you think Jack was successful in giving a gift to the princess? Why or why not?

_____

_____

_____

_____

_____

_____

_____

_____

_____

Quick Tip

Use these sentence starters to talk about Jack.

Jack was/was not successful because . . .

One reason for my opinion is . . .

CHECK IN   1   2   3   4

Money Then and Now

Literature Anthology:
pages 410–413

Earn and Spend

[1]   People earn money by working hard. They might have a job or invent something new. They might even start their own business. You might not be old enough to have a job, but there are many ways you can earn money. Lots of kids help their neighbors by raking leaves or walking dogs to earn cash. Some parents even give their kids an allowance in exchange for helping around the house.

[2]   What do you do with the money you earn? Well, you have a few choices. The easiest one is to spend the money you make on things you want or need. Spending money is easy. Learning to save money can be challenging.

Reread and use the prompts to take notes in the text.

In paragraph 1, **circle** the word *exchange*. **Underline** context clues that help you figure out the meaning of the word. What does *exchange* mean?

_____

_____

_____

Reread paragraph 2. **Draw a box around** the two different ways you can use money.

COLLABORATE

Talk with a partner about how the ways you can use money are different. **Make check marks** beside text evidence that describes how they are different.

Save and Donate

[3]   Saving money is important so that when you need it, you will have it. Many people put the money they want to save into a savings account at the bank. Then the bank pays interest, or money for every month the money stays at the bank.

[4]   Some people save some of their money but want to help others, too. Donating money means giving it to someone who needs it to do something good. Maybe you want to help groups who work with dogs and cats. Maybe you want to help people who are working to clean up the oceans. Making a donation helps pay for the things these people do.

In paragraph 3, **circle** the word *interest*. **Underline** context clues that can help you figure out its meaning. What does *interest* mean in this paragraph?

_____

_____

_____

COLLABORATE

Reread paragraph 4. **Draw boxes around** different groups you could donate money to. Talk with a partner about how your donations would help others. **Make a check mark** beside the statement that shows how.

How does the author help you understand what she thinks about saving and donating money?

Talk About It Reread the excerpt on page 55. Discuss with a partner how the author talks about saving and donating money. This will help you figure out the author's claim.

Cite Text Evidence How do you know what the author thinks about saving and donating money? Write text evidence in the chart.

Details

Author's Claim

Write I know what the author thinks about saving and donating

money because _____

_____

_____

CHECK IN 1 2 3 4

Author's Purpose

The author's purpose is the author's reason for writing. Authors will shape their writing to fit their purpose. For example, if an author is writing an expository text to inform readers about a topic, the author may use a formal voice, or personality. This means using good grammar, academic language, and a serious tone, or attitude.

FIND TEXT EVIDENCE

In paragraph 1 of the excerpt on page 55, the author writes, "Saving money is important so that when you need it, you will have it." The author's grammar and serious tone create a formal voice. This suits the author's purpose of informing the reader about money.

> Saving money is important so that when you need it, you will have it. Many people put the money they want to save into a savings account at the bank.

Your Turn Reread paragraph 2 on page 55.

- How do you know the author uses a formal voice? _____

_____

_____

Formal voice is created through complete sentences and good grammar. An informal voice is less serious and is used when speaking or writing to friends. When you write, use language that helps you form the appropriate voice for your purpose and audience.

CHECK IN 1 2 3 4

Ingram Publishing/SuperStock; Alcott, Louisa M. The Louisa Alcott Reader: A Supplementary Reader for the Fourth Year of School. Boston: Little, Brown, and Company, 1908.

? **How do the poet of "Here's a Nut" and the author of *Clever Jack Takes the Cake* help you visualize how the characters meet their needs?**

Talk About It Read the poem. Talk with a partner about how the squirrels in the poem get what they need.

Cite Text Evidence **Circle** clues in the poem that show that there are plenty of acorns. **Underline** how the squirrels get what they need.

Write I can visualize how Jack and the squirrels in the

poem get what they need because _____

_____

_____

_____

_____

_____

_____

Here's a Nut

Here's a nut, there's a nut;
Hide it quick away,
In a hole, under leaves,
To eat some winter day.
Acorns sweet are plenty,
We will have them all:
Skip and scamper lively
Till the last ones fall.

— Louisa May Alcott

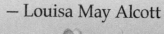

CHECK IN 1 2 3 4

My Goal I know how we get what we need.

Host an Awards Show

What did you learn about how people get what they need? Think about the characters you read about. What traits, or qualities, most helped the characters get what they needed?

1. Look at your Build Knowledge notes in your reader's notebook.

2. Choose three characters you read about. Pick a trait or skill for each character that they used to get what they needed.

3. On a sheet of paper, design an award to give to each character. Your award could be a trophy, ribbon, or some other prize. The award should recognize the character's trait or skill that you identified.

4. Beneath each award, write a sentence or two that describes why you're giving the character an award. Use new vocabulary words in your writing.

Think about what you learned in this text set. Fill in the bars on page 37.

Build Knowledge

Build Vocabulary

 Write new words you learned about energy and its different forms. Draw lines and circles for the words you write.

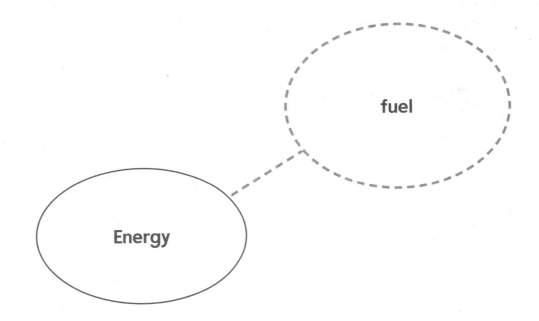

fuel

Energy

 Go online to **my.mheducation.com** and read the "Can You Hear Me?" Blast. Think about why learning about sound energy is important. Then blast back your response.

Think about what you already know. Fill in the bars. We all do better with practice.

What I Know Now

Key
1 = I do not understand.
2 = I understand but need more practice.
3 = I understand.
4 = I understand and can teach someone.

I can read and understand argumentative text.

1 > 2 > 3 > 4 >

I can use text evidence to respond to argumentative text.

1 > 2 > 3 > 4 >

I know about different kinds of energy.

1 > 2 > 3 > 4 >

STOP You will come back to the next page later.

Think about what you learned. Fill in the bars. Good job!

What I Learned

I can read and understand argumentative text.

1 > 2 > 3 > 4

I can use text evidence to respond to argumentative text.

1 > 2 > 3 > 4

I know about different kinds of energy.

1 > 2 > 3 > 4

My Goal: I can read and understand argumentative text.

TAKE NOTES

As you read, make note of interesting words and important information.

_____

_____

_____

_____

_____

_____

_____

_____

_____

This energetic snowboarder gets his power from the healthful foods he eats.

Essential Question

?

What are different kinds of energy?

Read why solar energy is a good source of power.

Corey Rich/Aurora Open/Corbis

Here Comes Solar Power

What do you have in common with a car and a factory? You both need **energy** to run. Energy keeps things moving.

Energy Today

You get your energy because you eat healthful foods. Most factories, homes, and cars get their energy from fossil fuels. Coal, petroleum, and natural gas are fossil fuels. They have been the **traditional**, or usual, energy **sources** for more than a century. Today, most of the energy we use in the United States comes from burning fossil fuels.

But these fuels come from deep under Earth's surface, and they are running out. They cannot be reused. Once a fossil fuel is gone, it's gone forever. So we need alternative energy sources to **replace** them. Scientists are looking for new, alternative sources of energy that won't run out. Solar power is one good alternative to fossil fuels.

FIND TEXT EVIDENCE 🔍

Read

Paragraphs 1–2

Cause and Effect

Underline what happens when you eat healthful foods. What signal word helps you know this?

_____

Paragraph 3

Ask and Answer Questions

What happens when a fossil fuel is gone?

_____

_____

Circle text evidence. Write your own question about fossil fuels.

_____

_____

Reread

Author's Craft

How does the author get you excited about solar power?

FIND TEXT EVIDENCE

Read

Paragraphs 1–2
Author's Claim
What is the author's claim in the heading about solar power?

Underline three reasons the author uses to support the claim.

Homophones
Draw a box around a word that sounds the same as *two.*

Write another one here. _____

Sidebar
Cause and Effect
What causes electricity to flow into buildings? **Circle** the cause.

Reread

Author's Craft

Why is "Solar Power Deserves Its Day in the Sun" a good heading for this section?

Solar Power Deserves Its Day in the Sun

Solar power is one source of **renewable** energy. And it is not expensive. Solar panels are getting cheaper to build and install every year. And sunlight is free, too! When people get energy from fossil fuels, they have to pay for all of the coal, oil, and natural gas that is burned up.

Solar power is also better for the environment, because it doesn't produce **pollution**. The pollution caused by fossil fuels can harm the quality of the air that we all need to breathe.

Solar panels are placed on the roof of a building.

How Solar Panels Work

Solar power is **natural**. That means it isn't made or changed by people. On a bright day, the Sun's rays hit solar panels and cause them to **produce** electricity. The electricity then flows into buildings. As a result, there is enough energy to cool or heat homes, and to power lights, stoves, and computers.

What Happens on a Rainy Day?

There are some drawbacks to solar energy. For one, if the Sun isn't shining, energy can't be produced. If it's nighttime or too cloudy, solar panels won't create any electricity. Scientists are designing more efficient batteries. These can charge up while the Sun is shining so that people can use solar power even after the Sun goes down. But those batteries can still run out if a lot of power is being used.

A Bright Future

Millions of people around the world use solar power to produce electricity for their homes and businesses. These people are finding that solar energy can do just about everything that fossil fuels do.

One day solar power might completely replace power from fossil fuels. That's good news for the environment!

Summarize

Review your notes on "Here Comes Solar Power." Summarize the text using the central idea and relevant details.

FIND TEXT EVIDENCE

Read

Paragraph 1

Cause and Effect

What is the effect of batteries that charge in the Sun?

_____

_____

Circle text evidence.

Paragraphs 2–3

Ask and Answer Questions

What could happen if solar power becomes more popular?

_____

_____

_____

Underline text evidence.

Reread

Author's Craft

How does the author help you understand what *drawbacks* are?

Vocabulary

Use the sentences to talk with a partner about each word. Then answer the questions.

energy

Good food gives Ron the **energy** he needs to play basketball with his friends.

Where do cars get their energy?

_____

_____

natural

Cotton is a **natural** material used to make clothes.

Name a natural material that is used in buildings.

_____

_____

> **Build Your Word List** Find the word *designing* on page 67. Write it in your reader's notebook. Use a word web to write more forms of the word. Use a dictionary to help.

pollution

Water **pollution**, such as garbage and chemicals, can harm animals.

Name something that causes air pollution.

_____

_____

produce

Solar panels can **produce** enough electricity to heat a whole house.

What word means the same as *produce*?

_____

_____

renewable

Trees are a **renewable** resource because more will always grow.

What does the word *renewable* mean?

_____

_____

replace

Soon Tina will **replace** her car with one that runs on electricity.

Name something that you can replace.

_____

_____

sources

Wind and solar power are two **sources** of energy we can use.

What are your energy sources?

_____

_____

traditional

Staying up late is a **traditional** way to celebrate New Year's.

What is another word for _traditional?_

_____

_____

Homophones

Homophones are words that sound the same but have different meanings and spellings. The words _sea_ and _see_ are homophones. Use context clues to figure out a homophone's meaning.

🔍 FIND TEXT EVIDENCE

I see the word need _on page 65._ Need _and_ knead _are homophones._ Need _means "to require something."_ Knead _means "to mix with your hands." I can use context clues to figure out what_ need _means. Here it means "to require."_

You both need energy to run.

Your Turn Use context clues to figure out what the word below means. Then write a homophone.

rays, page 66 _____

_____

CHECK IN ▷ 1 ▷ 2 ▷ 3 ▷ 4 ▷

Ask and Answer Questions

Asking yourself questions as you read helps you better understand what you are reading. Ask yourself questions as you read "Here Comes Solar Power." Then look for details to support your answers.

FIND TEXT EVIDENCE

Think of a question to ask about the section with the heading "Energy Today" on page 65. Then reread the section to answer it.

Page 65

You get your energy because you eat healthful foods. Most factories, homes, and cars get their energy from fossil fuels. Coal, petroleum, and natural gas are fossil fuels. They have been the **traditional,** or usual, energy **sources** for more than a century. Today, most of the energy we use in the United States comes from burning fossil fuels.

But these fuels come from deep under Earth's surface, and they are running out. They cannot be reused. Once a fossil fuel is gone, it's gone forever. So we need alternative energy

I have a question. What are fossil fuels? I read that most factories, homes, and cars run on fossil fuels. They come from deep under Earth's surface and are running out. Now I can answer my question. Fossil fuels are energy sources that come from the Earth and are not renewable.

Your Turn Reread page 66. Think of a question about solar energy and write it on the lines below. Talk with a partner about the answer.

CHECK IN 1 2 3 4

Author's Claim

"Here Comes Solar Power" is an **argumentative text**. Argumentative texts

- state a claim and persuade readers to agree with it
- support claims with evidence, such as facts and examples
- often include text features, such as headings and sidebars

🔍 FIND TEXT EVIDENCE

I can tell that "Here Comes Solar Power" is an argumentative text. The author states the claim that solar power is a useful energy source. This claim is supported by facts and examples. The author also includes headings and a sidebar to add meaning to the text.

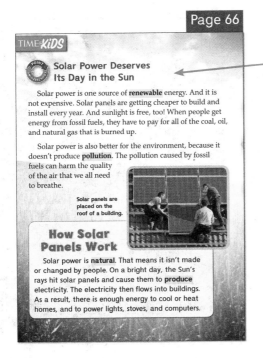

Page 66

TIME KIDS

Solar Power Deserves Its Day in the Sun

Solar power is one source of **renewable** energy. And it is not expensive. Solar panels are getting cheaper to build and install every year. And sunlight is free, too! When people get energy from fossil fuels, they have to pay for all of the coal, oil, and natural gas that is burned up.

Solar power is also better for the environment, because it doesn't produce **pollution**. The pollution caused by fossil fuels can harm the quality of the air that we all need to breathe.

Solar panels are placed on the roof of a building.

How Solar Panels Work

Solar power is **natural**. That means it isn't made or changed by people. On a bright day, the Sun's rays hit solar panels and cause them to **produce** electricity. The electricity then flows into buildings. As a result, there is enough energy to cool or heat homes, and to power lights, stoves, and computers.

Author's Claim

An author's claim is something the author thinks is true. The author can use text features, such as headings, to help readers better understand what he or she believes.

COLLABORATE

Your Turn Discuss how the heading "A Bright Future" on page 67 helps you understand the author's claim. Write your answer below.

_____

_____

_____

CHECK IN 1 ⟩ 2 ⟩ 3 ⟩ 4

Cause and Effect

A cause is why something happens. An effect is what happens. Describing causes and their effects is one way authors can structure a text. Understanding the relationship between events can help readers better understand a topic.

🔍 FIND TEXT EVIDENCE

On page 65, I read that we need to replace fossil fuels with alternative energy sources. This is the effect. The cause, or reason, for this is that once a fossil fuel is gone, it's gone forever. I can connect the cause and effect with the signal word so. Fossil fuels run out, so we need alternative energy sources.

Cause	→	Effect
Once a fossil fuel is gone, it's gone forever.	→	We need to replace fossil fuels with alternative energy sources.

Your Turn Reread "Here Comes Solar Power." Add more causes and effects to the graphic organizer. Remember to look for signal words.

Holger Burmeister/Alamy Stock Photo

CHECK IN 1 2 3 4

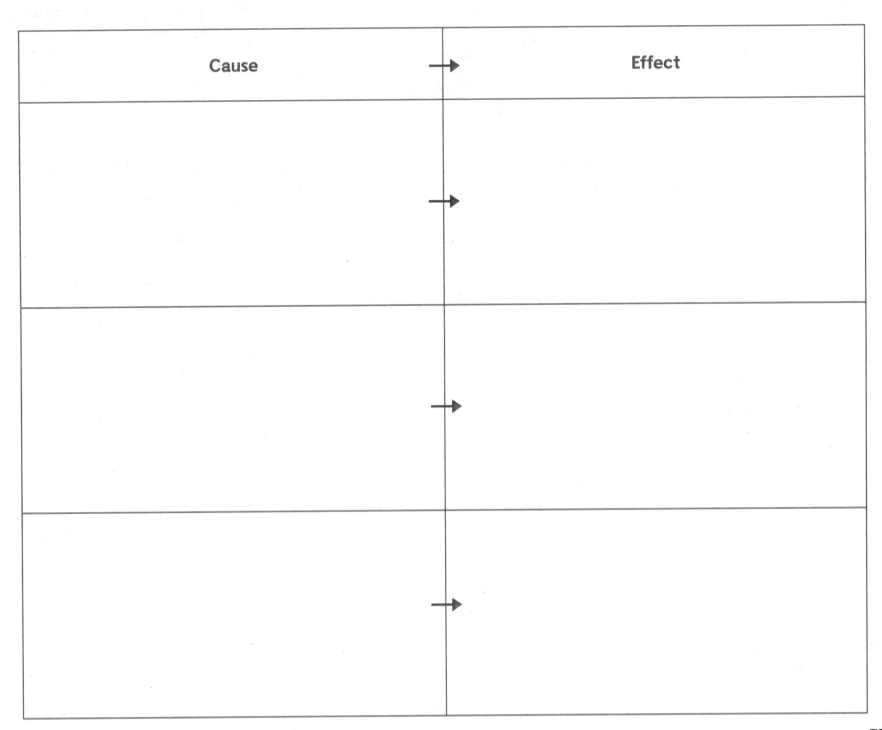

Cause	→	Effect
	→	
	→	
	→	

My Goal I can use text evidence to respond to argumentative text.

Respond to Reading

Talk about the prompt below. Use your notes and evidence from the text to support your answer.

Do you support the use of solar power? Use information from "Here Comes Solar Power" to explain your reasoning.

_____

_____

_____

_____

_____

_____

_____

_____

_____

Quick Tip

Use these sentence starters to talk about solar power.

I do/do not support the use of solar power because . . .

One reason for my opinion is . . .

Grammar Connections

As you write your response, use quotation marks when quoting the author's words. Remember that periods and commas go before the closing quotation mark, not after it.

CHECK IN 1 2 3 4

Sources of Energy

A chart like the one below is a good way to compare information. Follow the research process with a partner to learn about two kinds of energy. Create a chart to compare information you find.

	Is it renewable?	Does it pollute?
Natural Gas	No	Yes
Hydropower	Yes	No

Step 1 **Set a Goal** Select two forms of energy to research.

Step 2 **Identify Sources** Generate, or think of, questions about the energy sources you chose. Find books and reliable websites that will help you answer your questions.

Step 3 **Find and Record Information** Find answers to your questions. Record what you learn.

Step 4 **Organize and Combine Information** Plan your chart. Your energy sources should go in the first column. Your questions go in the first row. Use the sample chart as a model.

Step 5 **Create and Present** Complete your chart by filling in the answers to your questions. Present your chart to the class.

Quick Tip

As you research, ask questions that can be answered with *yes* or *no*. This will help you create a chart that makes it easy to see how things are alike or different.

CHECK IN 1 2 3 4

It's All in the Wind

*Literature Anthology:
pages 414–417*

 How does the author help you understand what the wind can do for people?

 Talk About It Reread page 415 in the **Literature Anthology**. Talk with a partner about what the wind can do for people.

Cite Text Evidence What text describes how people have used the wind? Record text evidence and say what it helps you understand.

Text Evidence	What I Understand

Write I understand how the wind helps people because the author

_____

_____

💡 **Evaluate Information**

The author claims that "People have been using wind as an energy source since ancient times." What evidence does the author use to support this claim? Is the evidence convincing?

CHECK IN 1 ⟩ 2 ⟩ 3 ⟩ 4 ⟩

Richard Ellis/Photodisc/Getty Images

? **How does the author use text features to help you understand how wind turbines can power a town?**

Talk About It Look at the diagram and photograph on **Literature Anthology** page 416. Talk about what these text features show.

Cite Text Evidence How do these text features help you understand how wind turbines provide electricity? Write how in the chart.

Text Feature	Clue	How It Helps

Write The text features help me understand how wind turbines can

power a town by _____

_____

_____

Quick Tip

When you reread, think about how each text feature adds meaning to the text. This can help you better understand the topic.

Make Inferences

An inference is a conclusion based on evidence. Use the photograph to make an inference about why some people don't want wind farms in their towns.

CHECK IN 〉 1 〉 2 〉 3 〉 4

Respond to Reading

COLLABORATE

Talk about the prompt below. Use your notes and evidence from the text to support your answer.

Do you support the use of wind energy? Why or why not? Use evidence from *It's All in the Wind* to explain your reasoning.

_____

_____

_____

_____

_____

_____

_____

_____

_____

Quick Tip

Use these sentence starters to talk about the prompt.

I do/do not support wind energy because . . .

One reason for my opinion is . . .

The author of It's All in the Wind *claims that . . .*

CHECK IN 1 2 3 4

Power for All

Literature Anthology:
pages 418–419

1   Every day, students in many countries are in a race against the Sun. Many don't have electricity. For this reason, they must do their homework during the daylight hours or use dangerous oil lamps or candlelight at night.

2   In Tsumkwe (CHOOM-kwee), a small town in Namibia, Africa, villagers were lucky. Until recently, they got all their electricity from a generator powered by oil. However, there were problems with the generator. It cost a lot of money. And it only produced electricity for three hours each day.

Reread and use the prompts to take notes in the text.

In paragraph 1, **underline** text evidence that explains why students are in a race against the Sun. Summarize why on the lines below.

_____

_____

_____

_____

Circle the words in paragraph 2 that help you understand where Tsumkwe is located.

COLLABORATE

Reread paragraph 2. Talk with a partner about why the generator didn't solve the villagers' problems. **Make check marks** in the margin next to text evidence that supports your discussion.

? How does the author's word choice help you visualize life without electricity?

 Talk About It Reread the excerpt on page 79. Talk with a partner about what life was like in Tsumkwe, Namibia.

Cite Text Evidence What words and phrases help you visualize what life would be like without electricity? Write text evidence in the chart.

Text Evidence	What I Visualize

Write The author helps me visualize what life would be like without

electricity by _____

_____

_____

Quick Tip

When you reread, you can visualize, or create pictures in your mind, by paying attention to interesting details.

 Make Inferences

An inference is a conclusion based on evidence. Use text evidence and what you know to make an inference about why oil lamps and candles could be dangerous.

CHECK IN 1 2 3 4

Text Features

Authors use text features, such as sidebars and maps, to help readers better understand a topic. Text features add meaning to a selection by giving information that is not in the main text. Authors may also use text features to give evidence in support of a claim.

FIND TEXT EVIDENCE

On page 419 of "Power for All" in the **Literature Anthology**, *the author includes a sidebar with ideas about how to save energy. By saying that the five ways are easy, the author is making a claim that she thinks saving energy is something everyone can do.*

> Here are five ‖easy‖ ways that you can save energy every day. Try them all!

Your Turn Reread the sidebar on page 419.

- What is another clue that tells you how the author feels about

  saving energy? _____

  _____

- How does the author support her claim?

  _____

Readers to Writers

When you write, think about using sidebars, photographs, captions, graphs, lists, headings, or maps to help your readers understand the topic better. If you want to share your opinion, these features can help you convince readers to agree with you.

CHECK IN 1 ⟩ 2 ⟩ 3 ⟩ 4

Dovydenko Yuliia/Shutterstock.com

? How do the painting below and the text features in *It's All in the Wind* and "Power for All" help you understand different kinds of energy?

Courtesy National Gallery of Art, Washington

Talk About It Look at the painting below and read the caption. With a partner, discuss how the ship is moving.

Cite Text Evidence Circle clues in the painting that show what makes the ship move. **Underline** a detail that suggests the ship is moving.

Write The painting and text features in the selections help me understand different types of energy because

_____

_____

_____

_____

_____

_____

_____

This oil painting of an American schooner was painted sometime during the nineteenth century by an unknown artist.

CHECK IN 〉 1 〉 2 〉 3 〉 4 〉

SHOW YOUR KNOWLEDGE

Plan a Science Lesson

Think about what you learned from the selections you read. What do you know about different kinds of energy? How are different kinds of energy useful or harmful? How can different kinds of energy affect our lives?

1 Look at your Build Knowledge notes in your reader's notebook.

2 Plan a short science lesson on energy that you could present to younger students in your school or community. What kinds of energy would you tell about in your lesson? How could you help students understand how energy affects our lives?

3 Create your science lesson. Write a few sentences that you could read to younger students to help them understand how different kinds of energy affect us. Include new vocabulary words that you learned.

Think about what you learned in this text set. Fill in the bars on page 63.

Think about what you already know. Fill in the bars. Now let's get started!

Key

1 = I do not understand.

2 = I understand but need more practice.

3 = I understand.

4 = I understand and can teach someone.

What I Know Now

I can write an opinion essay.

1 2 3 4

I can synthesize information from three sources.

1 2 3 4

STOP You will come back to the next page later.

What I Learned

I can write an opinion essay.

| 1 | 2 | 3 | 4 |

I can synthesize information from three sources.

| 1 | 2 | 3 | 4 |

WRITING

WRITE TO SOURCES

You will answer an opinion writing prompt using sources and a rubric.

ANALYZE THE RUBRIC

A rubric tells you what needs to be included in your writing.

Purpose, Focus, and Organization

Read the fourth bullet. What does "logical progression" mean?

_____

_____

Evidence and Elaboration

Read the fifth bullet. Underline the two kinds of vocabulary.

Academic language refers to words used in school, such as _analyze._ **Domain-specific language** refers to words used in a special subject. _Quotient_ is a domain-specific word in math.

What are two domain-specific words on the subject of voting?

_____

Opinion Writing Rubric

Purpose, Focus, and Organization • Score 4

- Stays focused on the purpose, audience, and task
- States the opinion in a clear way
- Uses transitional strategies, such as the use of signal, or linking, words and phrases, to show how ideas are connected
- **Has a logical progression of ideas**
- Begins with a strong introduction and ends with a conclusion

Evidence and Elaboration • Score 4

- Supports the opinion with convincing details
- Has strong examples of relevant evidence, or supporting details, with references to multiple sources
- Uses elaborative techniques, such as examples, definitions, and quotations from sources
- Uses precise language to express ideas clearly
- Uses appropriate academic and domain-specific language that matches the audience and purpose of the essay
- Uses different sentence types and lengths

Turn to page 240 for the complete Opinion Writing Rubric.

Valentain Jevee/Shutterstock

Opinion

Logical Progression of Ideas Writers of strong opinion essays clearly state their opinion. They develop their opinion with reasons that are supported by details from multiple sources. The ideas in the essay should move forward in a way that makes sense to help the reader better understand the opinion. Read the paragraph below. The two highlighted sentences show a logical progression of ideas.

> **Task**
>
> Writers who express their opinion have a task to explain their opinion in a logical way. One way to complete this task is to use signal words so the reader can easily follow their reasoning.

In Colonial America, most voters were 21 years old. Then in 1971 the voting law changed. As a result, 18-year-olds could vote in national elections. A year later, they voted for president for the first time. Now some people want to lower the voting age again. I think that's a bad idea. In my opinion, 16-year-olds should not vote for the president of the United States.

How does the writer clearly state his opinion?

____

____

Elaboration Writers use elaboration to make their essays stronger. This means taking time to further explain an idea. Including more details, examples, definitions, and quotations are ways to elaborate in your essay. In the paragraph above, **draw a box around** text that the writer uses to elaborate on the highlighted sentences.

ANALYZE THE STUDENT MODEL

Paragraph 1

Write a detail from Amir's introduction that caught your attention.

_____

_____

_____

The highlighted sentences show the start of Amir's logical progression of ideas. The signal word _then_ is a transition, or connection, between ideas. **Circle** more signal words and phrases that show a logical progression in paragraph 1.

Paragraph 2

Underline the claim in paragraph 2. What reasons does Amir give to support his claim?

_____

_____

_____

Student Model: Opinion Essay

Amir responded to the writing prompt: _Write an opinion essay about whether 16-year-olds should be allowed to vote for president of the United States._ Read Amir's essay below.

1   In Colonial America, most voters were 21 years old. Then in 1971 the voting law changed. As a result, 18-year-olds could vote in national elections. A year later, they voted for president for the first time. Now some people want to lower the voting age again. I think that's a bad idea. In my opinion, 16-year-olds should not vote for the president of the United States.

2   First, there has to be a good reason to change the voting age again. In 1971 there was. Eighteen-year-old soldiers were fighting a war in Vietnam. This war was very unpopular. Young soldiers asked a simple question: Should they fight when they couldn't vote for president? Many people agreed with them. They believed that changing the law was the right thing to do. But America is different today. I don't think there is an important reason to lower the voting age again.

3   Next, kids are not mature enough to vote at 16. The first source says that their brains are still developing. As a result, it's harder for them to make a good choice under pressure. Sometimes younger teens don't control their emotions very well.

Kids should be more mature before they take on more responsibilities. Other laws support this opinion. For example, 16- and 17-year-olds can't serve on juries. Why should voting be different?

4   Finally, I believe that 16-year-old kids aren't responsible enough to vote for president. The teenage writer of the third source agrees. Some students don't turn in their homework on time. Voting is a lot like homework. Voters must learn the facts about the candidates. Finding out that information isn't homework, but it is hard work. Unfortunately, many teens won't take the time. Instead, they will vote for a candidate because their parents or friends did. These teen voters might not think for themselves. But even if they don't vote, kids can still be politically active. They can join political clubs at school. Or, they can volunteer for candidates in their communities. Students can also march and demonstrate to support political causes.

5   For these reasons I believe that kids should not vote for president of the United States. Instead, they should be thinking about school and planning their futures. The more they know, the better informed they will be. When these students do vote, they will make good political choices.

OPINION ESSAY

Paragraph 3
Reread the third paragraph. **Underline** an example of elaboration that Amir uses. What claim does this elaboration support?

_____

_____

Paragraph 4
Find a signal word Amir uses to transition between ideas. What ideas does it connect?

_____

_____

_____

_____

Paragraph 5
Reread the conclusion. **Underline** how Amir concludes his essay.

Apply the Rubric

With a partner, use the rubric on page 86 to discuss why Amir scored a 4 on his essay.

Analyze the Prompt

Writing Prompt

Community service may soon be a requirement for students at your school. Write an essay giving your opinion about whether students should be required to do community service.

Purpose, Audience, and Task Reread the writing prompt. What is your purpose for writing? My purpose is to _____

_____

Who will your audience be? My audience will be _____

_____

What type of writing is the prompt asking for? _____

_____

Set a Purpose for Reading Sources Asking questions about whether community service should be required in school will help you set a purpose for reading. Before you read the passage set about community service, write a question here.

_____

_____

_____

Read the following passage set.

Volunteering Is a Choice

1   Some schools require that students do volunteer work. A requirement is something you have to do. Volunteering is a choice to use your energy for good. Requiring that students volunteer goes against the meaning of the word. **Volunteering should be a choice, not a chore.**

2   Most students have busy lives. They have homework. They may be members of sports teams or clubs. Some older students have after-school jobs or babysitting duties. If they have extra time, volunteering could be a great activity. But many students don't have extra time. Forcing them to volunteer is an added burden.

3   Some say that requiring children to volunteer builds a habit of volunteering. But the evidence does not support this. In 2013, Dr. Sara Helms studied volunteering at schools that require community service. Dr. Helms asks if students have to volunteer, do they think it's "community service, rather than just homework for school?" She found that younger students volunteered often. But older students volunteered less often.

4   Many students and parents are against required community service. They have argued that they have a right not to do work they do not want to do. The Constitution protects people from unpaid work. Is requiring students to volunteer going against their rights? In court cases, judges decided it was not. Still, many people think it is an unfair requirement.

FIND TEXT EVIDENCE

Paragraph 1
Read the highlighted opinion in paragraph 1.

Paragraph 2
Circle the reason the author gives to support the opinion.

Underline examples the author uses to support this reason.

Paragraphs 3–4
What are two reasons that the author gives against required volunteering?

_____

_____

_____

_____

_____

Take Notes Summarize the claim of the source. Include details that support the author's reasons for the claim.

WRITING

FIND TEXT EVIDENCE

Paragraph 5
Underline words and phrases that show how the ideas about volunteering logically progress.

Paragraph 6
What example is used to elaborate on the idea of service learning?

_____

_____

Paragraphs 7–8
List three advantages of service learning.

_____

_____

_____

Paragraph 9
Underline the author's claim in the conclusion.

Take Notes Summarize the claim of the source. Include details that support the author's reasons for the claim.

SOURCE 2

Serving and Learning

5   Good citizens work to improve their communities. One way to do this is through volunteering. People of all ages can do their part to help others. Volunteering can also be a learning experience. Because of this, many schools have made service learning a requirement.

6   Let's say you have learned about coastal pollution. The following week, your class cleans up a beach. Afterward, your class discusses the project's impact. This is an example of service learning. It blends education and community service. Through volunteering, students better understand what they learn in class.

7   Students often plan their own service-learning projects. With help from teachers or mentors, they propose a project and set learning goals. They can choose a cause that interests them. Once finished, students report on the outcome of their projects.

8   Research shows that service learning has many advantages. Students who participate in service learning projects score higher on state tests. They are more motivated to learn. They also learn about citizenship, teamwork, and leadership. They gain self-confidence. These are valuable skills and traits to take into adulthood.

9   More schools across America are introducing kids to service learning. Students and their communities will benefit as a result.

Getting INVOLVED

10   Community service is a great way to make a difference in the world. It is also great for you. According to the Corporation for National and Community Service, volunteering is good for your health. People who volunteer often are happier and live longer.

11   Even without the health benefits, most people agree that volunteering is a good thing. In fact, about 78 percent of young people think helping their community is important. But volunteering in America has gone down in recent years. How can more young people get involved in community service?

12   Many schools answer this question by assigning volunteer work. But this can result in uninterested students. They feel disconnected from the volunteer work if it is a school assignment. Schools need to understand their students' interests. That way they can connect students with volunteer work they truly care about.

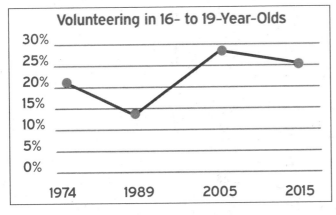

Although it has gone up since 1989, the volunteer rate of 16- to 19-year-olds has dipped in recent years.

FIND TEXT EVIDENCE 🔍

Paragraph 10
Circle the author's claim in the first paragraph.

Paragraphs 11–12
How have schools tried to solve the problem of the number of students volunteering going down?

_____

_____

_____

Line Graph
How did the volunteer rate change between 1989–2005?

_____

_____

_____

✏️ **Take Notes** Summarize the claim of the source. Include details that support the author's reasons for the claim.

I can synthesize information from three sources.

TAKE NOTES

Read the writing prompt below. Use the three sources, your notes, and the graphic organizer to plan a response.

Writing Prompt *Community service may soon be a requirement for students at your school. Write an essay giving your opinion about whether students should be required to do community service.*

Synthesize Information

Review the relevant evidence from each source. How does the evidence support your opinion about community service? Discuss your ideas with a partner.

Plan: Organize Ideas

Opinion	Supporting Claims
Students should/should not be required to do community service.	One reason for this is . . .

Relevant Evidence		
Source 1	Source 2	Source 3

Draft: Elaborative Techniques

Develop Your Claim Writers use facts, details, and examples to support their claims. They use definitions to explain terms readers might not know and interesting quotes to grab readers' attention. Include enough facts, details, examples, definitions, and quotes to help readers understand and be persuaded by your claim.

Reread "Volunteering Is a Choice" on page 91. Look for examples and definitions. Look for interesting quotations. Use text evidence to answer the questions below.

What is one interesting quote you read? Paraphrase it here.

Find one term that has a definition near it. Write the term and definition here.

Draft Use your graphic organizer and the examples above to write your draft in your writer's notebook. Before you start writing, review the rubric on page 86. Remember to use elaborative techniques.

CHECK IN 1 2 3 4

efiplus/Shutterstock.com

Revise: Peer Conferences

Review a Draft Listen actively to your partner. Take notes about what you liked and what was difficult to follow. Begin by telling what you liked. Use these sentence starters.

I like the evidence you used to support the claim because . . .
What did you mean by . . .
I think adding examples helps to . . .

After you finish giving each other feedback, reflect on the peer conference. What suggestion did you find to be the most helpful?

_____

_____

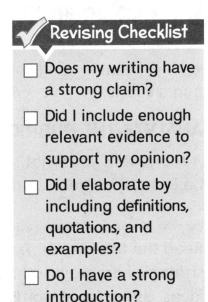

✓ Revising Checklist

- ☐ Does my writing have a strong claim?
- ☐ Did I include enough relevant evidence to support my opinion?
- ☐ Did I elaborate by including definitions, quotations, and examples?
- ☐ Do I have a strong introduction?
- ☐ Did I check my spelling and punctuation?

Revision Use the Revising Checklist to help you figure out what text you may need to move, elaborate on, or delete. After you finish writing your final draft, use the full rubric on pages 240–243 to score your essay.

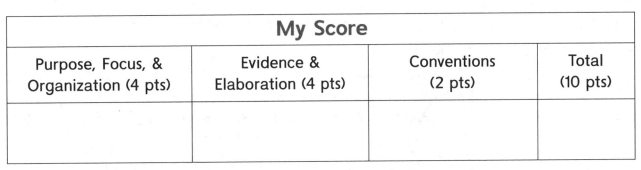

Next, you'll write an opinion essay on another topic.

My Score			
Purpose, Focus, & Organization (4 pts)	Evidence & Elaboration (4 pts)	Conventions (2 pts)	Total (10 pts)

WRITE TO SOURCES

You will answer an opinion writing prompt using sources and a rubric.

ANALYZE THE RUBRIC

A rubric tells you what needs to be included in your writing.

Purpose, Focus, and Organization

Read the third bullet. Transitional strategies are ways to help link ideas. Using signal words is a transitional strategy. How can this help readers?

_____

_____

Evidence and Elaboration

Read the fourth bullet. Underline how you can express your ideas.

Rewrite the following sentence with precise language to give more detail: *I read a good book.*

_____

_____

Opinion Writing Rubric

Purpose, Focus, and Organization • Score 4
• Stays focused on the purpose, audience, and task
• States the opinion in a clear way
• **Uses transitional strategies, such as the use of signal, or linking, words and phrases, to show how ideas are connected**
• Has a logical progression of ideas
• Begins with a strong introduction and ends with a conclusion

Evidence and Elaboration • Score 4
• Supports the opinion with convincing details
• Has strong examples of relevant evidence, or supporting details, with references to multiple sources
• Uses elaborative techniques, such as examples, definitions, and quotations from sources
• Uses precise language to express ideas clearly
• Uses appropriate academic and domain-specific language that matches the audience and purpose of the essay
• Uses different sentence types and lengths

Turn to page 240 for the complete Opinion Writing Rubric.

Valentain Jevee/Shutterstock

Transitional Strategies

Signal Words and Phrases A transitional strategy is a way for writers to smoothly shift from one idea to another. The use of signal, or linking, words and phrases is a common transitional strategy. Signal words and phrases include *however, next, as a result,* and *on the other hand*. Read the paragraph below. The signal word is highlighted.

> Have you ever wondered what powers the engine on the school bus or an airplane flying by? If you have, you may already know that most engines run on petroleum fuel. Petroleum is a useful fossil fuel that is found beneath Earth's surface. **However**, fossil fuel is not a renewable energy source.

A signal word helps the writer transition between, or connect, two ideas. What ideas does the writer connect with the word *however* in the paragraph above?

_____

_____

Strong Introduction Successful opinion essays have a strong introduction. The introduction should grab the reader's attention.

Read the paragraph above. Underline how the writer grabs your attention. Describe how the writer does it.

_____

Audience

Writers have an audience in mind when they write. They make choices about what to include based on their audience. Reread the paragraph about fossil fuels. Who is the audience?

WRITING

ANALYZE THE STUDENT MODEL

Paragraph 1

Write an interesting detail from Makayla's introduction.

_____

_____

A transitional strategy in the first paragraph is highlighted. Makayla expresses her opinion with the word "especially." She is stating that there are other fuel sources, but renewable ones are especially important.

Paragraph 2

What is an example of precise language that Makayla uses to express her ideas more clearly?

_____

_____

Circle an example of a domain-specific vocabulary word.

Student Model: Opinion Essay

Makayla responded to the writing prompt: *Write an opinion essay about whether renewable or nonrenewable energy is the better choice.* Read Makayla's essay below.

1   Have you ever wondered what powers the engine on the school bus or an airplane flying by? If you have, you may already know that most engines run on petroleum fuel. Petroleum is a fossil fuel. It's found in rocks beneath Earth's surface. It is called a fossil fuel because it is made from decaying organisms from millions of years ago. The fuel is made from fossils. However, fossil fuel is not a renewable energy source. That means we will run out of it someday. It is important to find different energy sources, especially ones that are renewable. Ethanol fuel may be a solution.

2   The United States has already started using ethanol fuel in cars. Ethanol can be used in any car or truck that runs on gasoline. There is no special equipment needed. Almost all the gasoline sold here is mixed with 10 percent ethanol. Ethanol fuel is made from sugar from plants such as corn and sugar cane. Plants are renewable. The crops used to make ethanol fuel can be regrown. And because ethanol is already in gasoline, it can be slowly increased to 100 percent.

3   Ethanol fuel is a good option, but it is not a perfect solution. Burning ethanol fuel is much better for the environment than burning fossil fuel, but there are some negative effects. Growing all the crops needed to produce ethanol is not easy. A lot of land and water is needed. They are valuable resources, too. However, growing ethanol crops creates much needed jobs in rural areas. Another argument is that it seems like a waste of food. Crops grown for ethanol could be used to feed people. One solution to that is to use ethanol made from grass, wood, and other plants that humans don't eat.

4   As time goes by, I believe science will find ways to work around these problems. More effort should be put into studying ethanol more closely. We are using up all our fossil fuels. We are hurting our environment by burning fossil fuels, too. We have to do more to make sure the world keeps moving.

(bkgd)Titus Group/Shutterstock, (paperclips)Oleksandr Derevianko/Shutterstock, (kids)wavebreakmedia/Shutterstock

Paragraph 3

Reread the third paragraph. **Underline** how Makayla elaborates on the negative effects of ethanol fuel. What reasons does Makayla give to convince the reader that ethanol fuel is still better than fossil fuels?

_____

_____

_____

Paragraph 4

What is an example of a signal word or phrase Makayla uses to connect her ideas?

_____

_____

Underline Makayla's strong concluding statement.

Apply the Rubric

With a partner, use the rubric on page 98 to discuss why Makayla scored a 4 on her essay.

I can write an opinion essay.

Analyze the Prompt

Writing Prompt

Write an opinion essay for your local newspaper about whether your town should choose wind or solar power as its energy source.

Purpose, Audience, and Task Reread the writing prompt. What is your purpose for writing? My purpose is to _____

_____

Who will your audience be? My audience will be _____

_____

What type of writing is the prompt asking for? _____

_____

Set a Purpose for Reading Sources Asking questions about whether solar or wind power is a better source of energy for your town will help you figure out your purpose for reading. Before you read the passage set about solar and wind energy, write a question here.

_____

_____

_____

Read the following passage set.

Wind Energy is for Everyone

1   The wind howls. It lifts a kite high into the air. It bends trees. It can also turn the blades of a wind turbine. This converts wind energy to electricity. People can use the energy to power lights, TVs, cars, and more. **Wind energy is a great source of energy.**

2   It is fairly easy to harness wind power. William Kamkwamba lives in the country of Malawi. He built a wind turbine. His wind turbine powers his family's home. Wind turbines can be big or small. They can be made out of metal, wood, or other materials. A single person, like William, can build a turbine. Then, even while the person is at work or at school, the wind turbine will convert wind energy to electricity. Once the person returns home, he or she can use this electricity. It's as easy as that!

3   According to the American Wind Energy Association, wind turbines work best in places where the wind blows at least six miles per hour. As it turns out, this happens in many places in the United States and around the world. Countries can build groups of wind turbines called wind farms. The energy from them can be used by those countries, but it can also be shared with other countries.

4   Wind power is amazing. All that is needed is a wind turbine and enough wind to spin the turbine's blades. Then the energy obtained from the wind can be used or shared around the world.

FIND TEXT EVIDENCE

Paragraph 1
Read the highlighted claim in paragraph 1.

Paragraph 2
Underline reasons why wind power is a good source of energy.

Paragraph 3
Circle a signal phrase the author uses to connect ideas.

What ideas are connected?

_____

_____

_____

_____

Paragraph 4
Draw a box around the author's claim.

Take Notes Summarize the source. Give examples of details that support the reasons for the author's claim.

FIND TEXT EVIDENCE

Paragraph 5
Underline the claim in paragraph 5.

Paragraph 6
Circle the words and phrases that help the ideas logically progress through paragraph 6.

Paragraph 7
Underline the claim. Write a reason that supports the claim.

_____

_____

Photograph and Caption
Write something you learned from the photograph and caption that you did not learn from the essay.

_____

_____

Take Notes Summarize the source. Give examples of details that support the author's reasons for the claim.

SOURCE 2

The Incredible Power of Solar Energy

5   The Sun is very powerful. It warms the oceans. It heats the air. The Sun produces enormous amounts of energy each day. Researchers have calculated that the Sun produces more energy in one hour than all the people on Earth use in a year. Because of this, I agree with many researchers that it is possible to supply everyone's energy needs by using solar power. It is possible that just a small percentage of Earth would need to have solar panels to provide all the energy humans use. The Sun is just that powerful!

6   Some parts of the Earth get more sunlight than other parts of the Earth. For example, the equator gets lots of sunlight all year round. But the Sun reaches everywhere on Earth. That means that everyone can harness the energy of the Sun.

7   The Sun is incredibly powerful. It produces more energy than humans could ever use. Because of that, the Sun is an ideal source of energy.

Researchers have created sidewalks with solar panels. These panels absorb the Sun's energy. The energy can be used to power other things.

Martin Bond/Alamy Stock Photo

Wind AND Solar
THE PERFECT COMBINATION

8   People around the world are concerned about energy. Some researchers think that common sources of energy, such as oil and gas, are getting used up. They are also concerned that they are polluting our air, soil, and water. Many people around the world want our air, soil, and water to be clean. They want sources of energy that are reliable. Wind and solar energy are great choices.

9   Some sources of energy are limited, such as oil and gas. These sources are called nonrenewable. That means that they can be used up. Other sources are unlimited, such as wind and solar. These sources are called renewable. They cannot be used up. Earth naturally creates the wind, and the Sun always shines. As people use renewable energy, Earth makes more.

10   According to the United States Environmental Protection Agency, more than 100 million people in the United States live in areas with high levels of air pollution. Other research has shown a rise in soil and water pollution. Researchers think much of this pollution is from using oil and gas. But wind and solar energy do not release harmful chemicals. They are "clean" energy sources.

11   Wind and solar are both renewable and clean energy sources. By using these sources, people could limit pollutants while also getting all their energy needs met.

OPINION ESSAY

FIND TEXT EVIDENCE

Paragraph 8
Underline the claim.

Write two reasons the author has for this claim.

_____

Paragraph 9
Circle the two definitions that elaborate on the sources of energy.

Write the words and their definitions.

_____

_____

_____

Paragraphs 10–11
Why are wind and solar energy known as "clean" energy sources?

_____

_____

Take Notes Summarize the source. Include reasons that develop the author's claim.

WRITING

My Goal I can synthesize information from three sources.

TAKE NOTES

Read the writing prompt below. Use the three sources, your notes, and the graphic organizer to plan your essay.

Writing Prompt *Write an opinion essay for your local newspaper about whether your town should choose wind or solar power as its energy source.*

Synthesize Information

Review the relevant evidence you recorded from each source. How does the information support your opinion about energy sources? Discuss your ideas with a partner.

CHECK IN 1 2 3 4

Plan: Organize Ideas

Introduction State the opinion.	I believe wind/solar power is the best source of energy.

Body Supporting Claims	One reason for this is . . .

Conclusion Restate the opinion.	

Valentain Jevee/Shutterstock

Relevant Evidence		
Source 1	**Source 2**	**Source 3**

Draft: Word Choice

Precise Nouns A noun is a person, place, or thing. For example, *Tallahassee, Africa*, and *ethanol* are all nouns. Precise nouns are more specific. For example, *novel* is more specific than *book*. Writers make their ideas clearer by using precise nouns.

Reread the essay "Wind and Solar: The Perfect Combination" on page 105. Talk with a partner about any words you might choose to replace with a more precise noun. You can use a thesaurus to help you find a more precise noun. A thesaurus is a book or Internet source that lists synonyms.

Write your word and the more precise noun you would replace it with. Explain why you chose that word.

_____

_____

_____

_____

_____

Draft Use your graphic organizer and what you learned above to write your draft in your writer's notebook. Before you start writing, review the rubric on page 98. Remember to indent each paragraph.

Quick Tip

Use precise nouns to help your readers visualize people, places, and objects in your opinion essay.

CHECK IN 1 〉 2 〉 3 〉 4 〉

Revise: Peer Conferences

COLLABORATE

Review a Draft Listen actively to your partner. Take notes about what you liked and what was difficult to follow. Begin by telling what you liked. Use these sentence starters.

I like the evidence you used to support the opinion because . . .
What did you mean by . . .
I think adding signal words would help to . . .

After you finish giving each other feedback, reflect on the peer conference. What suggestion did you find to be the most helpful?

_____

_____

Revising Checklist

☐ Does my writing have a strong claim?

☐ Did I include enough relevant evidence to support my claim?

☐ Did I use transitional strategies to show the connections between ideas?

☐ Do I have a strong introduction?

☐ Did I check my spelling and punctuation?

Revision Use the Revising Checklist to help you figure out what text you may need to move, elaborate on, or delete. After you finish writing your final draft, use the full rubric on pages 240–243 to score your essay.

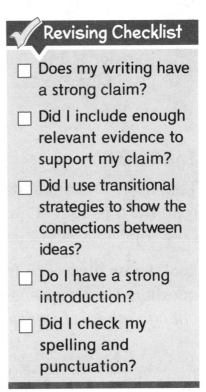

Turn to page 85. Fill in the bars to show what you learned.

My Score			
Purpose, Focus, & Organization (4 pts)	Evidence & Elaboration (4 pts)	Conventions (2 pts)	Total (10 pts)

My Goal I can read and understand science texts.

TAKE NOTES

Take notes and annotate as you read the passages "Catching the Cold" and "Watery Science."

Look for an answer to the question. *How does energy change other substances?*

_____

_____

_____

_____

_____

_____

_____

PASSAGE 1 **EXPOSITORY TEXT**

Catching the Cold

Have you ever wondered about the temperatures hot and cold? Think about hot for a moment. You can rub your hands together and immediately feel warmth. Moving your hands together quickly creates friction. Try it! Friction is the term for when things move against each other and heat up.

Now think about cold. Can you make cold like you can make heat? Way back in the 1600s, scientists were puzzled about what made things cold. They thought cold was an invisible thing that entered your body or your house.

English scientist Robert Boyle wanted to know what makes things cold. He designed a simple experiment. He filled a bucket with water. Then he carefully weighed the bucket and recorded the weight in his notes. Boyle then placed the bucket outside in the freezing cold. The next morning, the water was frozen solid. Boyle quickly took the bucket inside to weigh it.

Can you guess what happened? That's right! The bucket weighed the same. Boyle had proven that nothing was added to the water to make it freezing cold. So, what froze the water? Where cold came from still remained a mystery.

Around the same time, French scientist Guillaume Amontons had another way of looking at the cold. Amontons performed a lot of experiments with heat and thermometers.

He noticed that when a thermometer was heated, the mercury inside would rise. What caused that? He thought it was tiny invisible springs inside the mercury. When the mercury was heated, he thought the springs stretched out and took up more space. Amontons then had a breakthrough! Cold must be when the springs shrink down and take up less space.

Amontons's ideas were accurate. But instead of springs, there are atoms that make up everything. When something heats up, the atoms move quickly. The atoms move apart and take up more space. When things are cold, the atoms slow down and move closer together. They take up less space. Amontons had solved the mystery of what makes things cold. Cold is the slowing down of an object's atoms.

PASSAGE 2 EXPOSITORY TEXT

Watery Science

You know what cold feels like. You've touched an ice cube, or you may have played in the snow. An ice cube is about 32 degrees Fahrenheit. It's the temperature when liquid water freezes into solid ice. It is the temperature at which water changes states from a liquid to a solid.

What does changing states mean? It doesn't mean packing up and moving! A state is the form something takes. There are three states of matter: solid, liquid, and gas.

TAKE NOTES

oleandra/Shutterstock

TAKE NOTES

_____

_____

_____

_____

_____

_____

_____

_____

_____

_____

_____

_____

_____

_____

_____

Water is a great substance to study. It can be found in all three states of matter. First, water naturally exists as a liquid. Second, when water freezes, it turns into ice, which is a solid. Third, when water boils, it evaporates and turns into steam, which is a gas. How does water do it?

Like everything else in the universe, water is made of atoms. Boiling water turns it into steam. The heat makes the atoms move around very quickly. The atoms spread far apart. The heat changes water's state from a liquid to a gas. The atoms in liquid water are also moving around quickly. They slide around. This is the slippery wetness of liquid water. The atoms in ice move very slowly, making water freeze to become a solid.

The atoms themselves in water never change. They change states, or forms, by how much energy they have. High energy, or heat, turns water into a gas. Low energy turns water into a solid. Normal room temperature energy gives us liquid water.

Designua/Shutterstock

COMPARE THE PASSAGES

Review your notes from "Catching the Cold" and "Watery Science." Then create a Venn diagram like the one below. Use the diagram to record how information in the passages is alike and different.

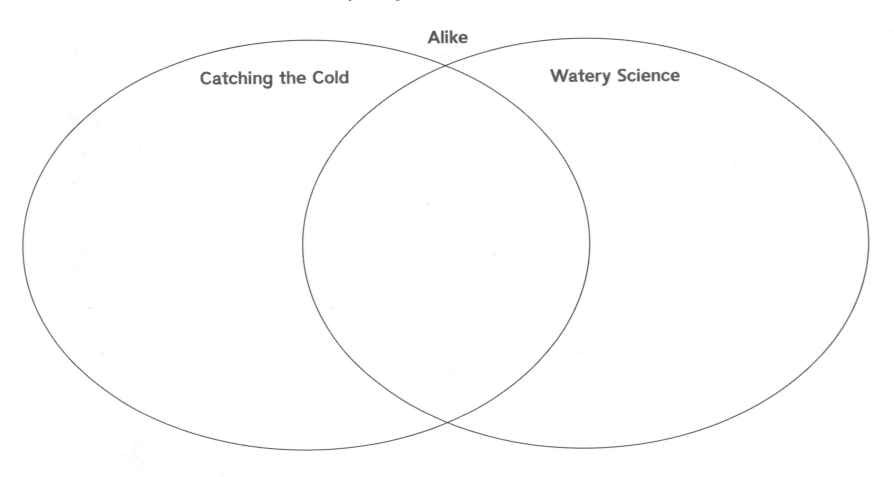

Alike

Catching the Cold

Watery Science

Synthesize Information

Think about both texts. How has studying water helped scientists understand more about energy and the states of matter?

CHECK IN 〉 1 〉 2 〉 3 〉 4 〉

EXPLORING WATERY STATES

You've learned about different states of matter. Now it's time to explore water in two of its states: solid and liquid. You're going to explore water and ice in three ways: temperature, mass, and volume.

Gather the materials: water, two freezer-safe measuring cups, a scale, a freezer, and a thermometer.

Temperature is how hot or cold something is. You can measure temperature with a thermometer.

Pour one cup of water into each of your measuring cups. Place one of the cups of water in the freezer. After the water has frozen, use the thermometer to take the temperature of the water in one cup and ice in the other. Record the temperatures in the chart.

	Temperature
Water	
Ice	

Which is warmer? By how many degrees?

_____

_____

Mass is the amount of matter, or substance, in an object. You can measure an object's mass by weighing it on a scale. Weigh your cup of liquid water on the scale. Record the weight you see in the chart below. Then weigh the cup of frozen water and record its weight.

	Weight
Water	
Ice	

Were their weights the same or different? Why do you think?

Volume is how much space something takes up. Look at your cup of liquid water. Record the number on the line where the water comes to. Then look at your cup of frozen water. Record the number that lines up with the surface of the ice.

	Volume
Water	
Ice	

What do you notice? Do the ice and water come to the same level, or is one higher than the other?

My Goal I can read and understand social studies texts.

TAKE NOTES

Take notes and annotate as you read the passages "Leading the Dance" and "Sharing Culture Through Dance."

Look for an answer to the question. *How do artists contribute to our world?*

_____

_____

_____

_____

_____

_____

_____

PASSAGE 1

EXPOSITORY TEXT

Leading the Dance

Katherine Dunham was many things. She was a dancer. She was a choreographer, which means she decided how dancers move during a performance. She was a writer and a researcher. Above all, Katherine Dunham was a leader. She created new opportunities for talented black artists.

Dunham was born in Chicago in 1909. She became interested in dance as a teenager and studied ballet. She went on to study anthropology at the University of Chicago. Anthropology is the study of people and their cultures. She focused her studies on dance styles with African roots. In 1935, Dunham went to the Caribbean to do dance research.

Back in the United States, Dunham formed a troupe, or group, of black dancers. They performed dances inspired by her research in the Caribbean and by African dance. Audiences around the world enjoyed their performances. It was a breakthrough for black artists.

Katherine Dunham (front) was a pioneer of modern dance.

New York Daily News Archive/New York Daily News/Getty Images

Dunham developed special ways of moving and dancing. She opened schools to teach her techniques. Some of her students became new leaders in modern dance and theater.

Dunham helped many people during her ninety-six years of life. She taught children in poor communities. She funded a hospital in Haiti. She spoke up for people who were being mistreated. The creative movement she started goes on.

PASSAGE 2 EXPOSITORY TEXT

Sharing Culture Through Dance

Alvin Ailey was a dancer and choreographer. He was born in Texas in 1931. The dance company he founded helped make modern dance popular in the United States.

Ailey moved to Los Angeles when he was eleven years old. He began to study dance with Lester Horton as a teenager. Horton led a company of dancers from many backgrounds. He was one of the first choreographers to do so.

Ailey formed the Alvin Ailey American Dance Theater in 1958 in New York. The company started as a group of seven black dancers. They performed modern dance classics and Ailey's works. Katherine Dunham's work was featured. Dunham had inspired Ailey to dance when he was young.

TAKE NOTES

_____

_____

_____

_____

_____

_____

_____

_____

_____

_____

_____

_____

_____

_____

_____

TAKE NOTES

When Ailey's dance company began, the civil rights movement was growing. Ailey's work often celebrated African American culture and life. In this way, Ailey helped African Americans fight for equal rights.

Ailey's greatest work may be *Revelations*. It is a dance program in three parts. The dances are set to African American church music and traditional songs. *Revelations* expresses powerful emotions, from sadness to joy. The work was first performed in 1960. It is still performed around the world.

By 1970, Ailey's company was an important part of American culture. Ailey died in 1989, but his work lives on. And so does the Alvin Ailey American Dance Theater. In 2014, President Obama gave Alvin Ailey the Medal of Freedom. This award honors great citizens.

Members of the Alvin Ailey American Dance Theater performing in Germany.

COMPARE THE PASSAGES

Review your notes from "Leading the Dance" and "Sharing Culture Through Dance." Then create a Venn diagram. Use the diagram to record how information in the two passages is alike and different.

Alike

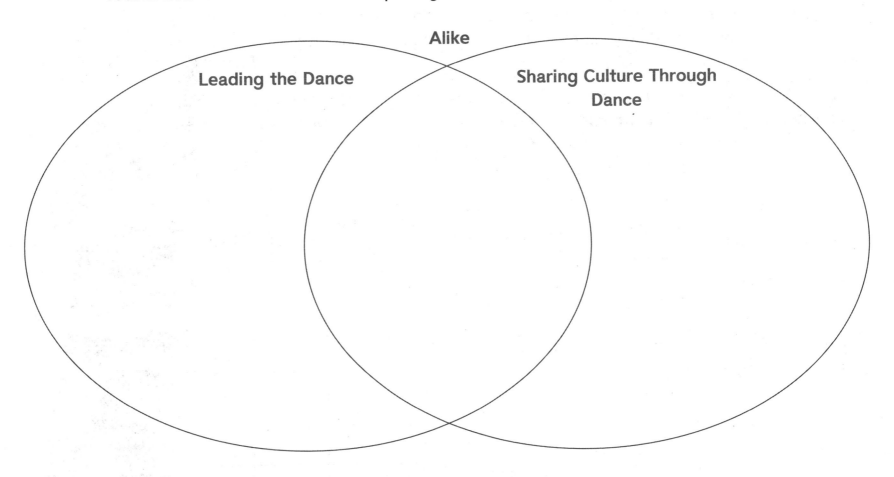

Leading the Dance

Sharing Culture Through Dance

💡 **Synthesize Information**

Think about both texts. How can dance and other forms of art help people share their culture with others?

TELL A STORY WITH DANCE

You've read about Katherine Dunham and Alvin Ailey. These dancers and choreographers expressed feelings through dance. They told stories with dance. Think about a story that you read in this unit, or another story you know. What feelings are described in the story? How could you show that part of the story without words, using movements?

Work with a partner to create movements to tell part of a story you both know. Create at least two movements. Use the chart below to organize your ideas. A sample is shown.

Name of Story	Character	What Happened to the Character	How the Character Feels	Dance Movement
"Clever Jack Takes the Cake"	Jack	Jack was invited to cut the Princess's birthday cake.	proud	smiles and bows deeply

Once you have thought of your dance movement, share it with the class. Ask them to guess what emotion you are expressing.

Ron Krisel/Getty Images

Reflect on Your Learning

Talk About It Reflect on what you learned in this unit. Then talk with a partner about how you did.

I am really proud of how I can _____

_____

_____

_____

Something I need to work more on is _____

_____

_____

_____

> Share a goal you have with a partner.

My Goal Set a goal for Unit 6. In your reader's notebook, write about what you can do to get there.

Build Knowledge

Essential Question
Why are goals important?

Build Vocabulary

Write new words you learned about goals and why they are important. Draw lines and circles for the words you write.

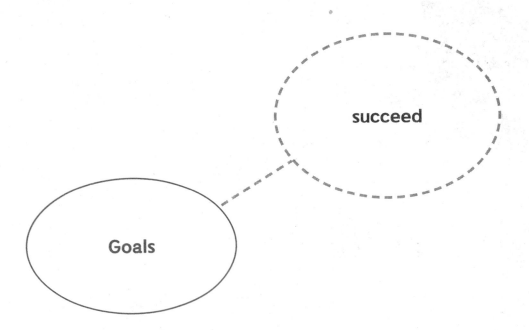

succeed

Goals

Go online to **my.mheducation.com** and read the "Mission: Juno" Blast. Think about why it's important for scientists to set goals for exploring space. Then blast back your response.

Think about what you already know. Fill in the bars. You'll learn more with practice.

Key

1 =	I do not understand.
2 =	I understand but need more practice.
3 =	I understand.
4 =	I understand and can teach someone.

What I Know Now

I can read and understand a biography.

| 1 | 2 | 3 | 4 |

I can use text evidence to respond to a biography.

| 1 | 2 | 3 | 4 |

I know why goals are important.

| 1 | 2 | 3 | 4 |

 You will come back to the next page later.

Think about what you learned. Fill in the bars. What is getting easier for you?

What I Learned

I can read and understand a biography.

1 2 3 4

I can use text evidence to respond to a biography.

1 2 3 4

I know why goals are important.

1 2 3 4

My Goal I can read and understand a biography.

TAKE NOTES

As you read, make note of interesting words and important information.

ROCKETING INTO SPACE

Essential Question

Why are goals important?

Read how one man used his education and experience to reach his goals.

When James A. Lovell Jr. was a boy, he loved to build rockets and launch them into the sky. But his dreams went a lot farther than his rockets. Like many boys who grew up in the 1930s, James dreamed of being a pilot. And as he watched his rockets soar, he knew someday he would, too.

High-Flying Dreams

James was born in Cleveland, Ohio, in 1928. He worked hard in school and planned to go to a special college to study **astronomy** and rockets. Unfortunately, he didn't have enough money to attend. James had to figure out another way to reach his **goal**.

James was **motivated** to find a way to fly rockets. So, he went to college near his home for two years and then signed up for flight training at the United States Naval Academy. After four years at the academy, James joined the United States Navy and became a **professional** naval test pilot. His job was to fly planes before anyone else was allowed to fly them.

James A. Lovell Jr. became an astronaut in 1962. He flew four space missions.

Time Life Pictures/NASA/The LIFE Picture Collection/Getty Images

FIND TEXT EVIDENCE 🔍

Read

Paragraphs 1–2
Key Words
Find the key word. Write it below.

_____

Underline details that show how the key word is important to understanding James Lovell.

Paragraph 3
Reread
What did James do after he joined the Navy?

_____

_____

_____

Circle text evidence.

Reread

Author's Craft

How does the author help you understand how motivated James Lovell was to become an astronaut?

SHARED READ

FIND TEXT EVIDENCE

Read

Paragraph 1
Greek and Latin Roots
Underline the word *astronaut.*
What does an astronaut do?

Paragraphs 2–4
Central Idea and Details
Draw a box around details that tell what went wrong with the Apollo 13 mission. How did the astronauts solve their problem?

Photographs
Circle how NASA's team helped.

Reread

Author's Craft

Why is "Big Challenges" a good heading for this section?

Pilot to Astronaut

As a pilot, James spent more than half of his flying time in jets. He taught other pilots how to fly. He also worked as a **specialist** in air flight safety. Soon, the National Aeronautics and Space Administration, or NASA, put out a call for astronauts. James applied for the job because he had all the **essential** skills needed to fly into space. As a result, NASA chose him. By 1962, James Lovell was an astronaut! He had finally reached his goal.

Big Challenges

James flew on three space missions, and then in April 1970 he became **commander** of the Apollo 13 mission. This was a big responsibility and a great honor. This was also one of the biggest challenges of James's life.

Apollo 13 was supposed to land on the Moon. Two days after leaving Earth, however, the **spacecraft** had a **serious** problem. One of its oxygen tanks exploded. The crew did not have enough power or air to breathe. They could not make it to the Moon.

James **communicated** with the experts at NASA. No one knew what to do at first. Then the team on the ground did some **research** and came up with a solution. The astronauts followed the team's directions and built an invention using plastic bags, cardboard, and tape. It worked! It cleaned the air in the spacecraft. But the next problem was even bigger. How were the astronauts going to get back to Earth?

NASA's team works to solve Apollo 13's problem.

A Job Well Done

The NASA team decided the astronauts would use the lunar, or moon, module as a lifeboat. James and the other two astronauts climbed into the smaller spacecraft and shut the hatch tight. They moved away from the main spaceship. With little power, water, food, or heat, the astronauts listened carefully to the team at NASA.

The trip back to Earth was dangerous and scary. For almost four days, the astronauts traveled in the cramped capsule. They were cold, thirsty, and hungry. Then, with millions of people watching on television, the module fell to Earth.

Years later, James Lovell said that Apollo 13 taught him how important it was for people to work together. His favorite memory was when the capsule splashed down in the Pacific Ocean and he knew they were safe.

A Dream Come True

DID YOU EVER DREAM OF GOING INTO SPACE? CHECK OUT SPACE CAMP!

Space camps have been around for more than 30 years. They make science, math, and technology exciting so kids will want to learn more. And like the NASA training programs, these camps teach the importance of teamwork and leadership.

The Apollo 13 crew splashed down safely on April 17, 1970.

Summarize

Review your notes. Summarize "Rocketing into Space" using the central idea and relevant details.

FIND TEXT EVIDENCE

Read

Paragraphs 1-2

Reread

Why was the trip back to Earth so difficult?

_____

_____

Circle text evidence.

Paragraph 3

Central Idea and Details

Underline a detail that tells what Apollo 13 taught Lovell. What is the central idea of this section?

_____

_____

_____

Reread

Author's Craft

How does the author help you understand how James Lovell felt about the Apollo 13 mission?

Vocabulary

Use the sentences to talk with a partner about each word. Then answer the questions.

communicated

Mora and her friends **communicated** by writing e-mails to each other.

What are some ways you have communicated with your friends?

_____

_____

essential

A toothbrush is an **essential** tool for cleaning teeth.

What is an essential tool you use in the classroom?

_____

_____

goal

Nick reached his **goal** and learned to swim.

Tell about a goal you have.

_____

_____

motivated

Katie was **motivated** to learn to play her guitar, so she practiced every day.

What is something you are motivated to learn how to do?

_____

_____

professional

Ted works as a **professional** musician.

Name a professional athlete you know about.

_____

_____

Build Your Word List Reread the first paragraph on page 127. Draw a box around the word *soar*. In your reader's notebook, make a list of synonyms and antonyms for *soar*. Use a thesaurus to help you find more.

research

Melanie's mom is a scientist, and she uses a microscope to do **research**.

What animal would you like to research?

_____

_____

serious

Winnie pays attention because she is **serious** about getting good grades.

What is something you are serious about?

_____

_____

specialist

Dr. Morrison is a **specialist** in sports medicine.

What is something you know a lot about and could be a specialist in?

_____

_____

Greek and Latin Roots

Many words have roots that come from older languages, such as Greek and Latin. The Greek root *astro* means "star," and *naut* means "ship." The Latin root *luna* means "moon."

FIND TEXT EVIDENCE

On page 127, I see the word astronomy. *I remember that* astro *is a Greek root that means "star." This helps me understand that* astronomy *means "the study of stars."*

He worked hard in school and planned to go to a special college to study astronomy and rockets.

Your Turn Use the Latin root *luna* to figure out the meaning of the word below.

lunar, page 129 _____

_____

CHECK IN 1 2 3 4

Reread

Stop and think about the text as you read. Are there new facts and ideas? Do they make sense? Reread to make sure you understand.

🔍 **FIND TEXT EVIDENCE**

Reread "High-Flying Dreams" on page 127. Do you understand what James A. Lovell Jr. did to become a pilot?

Quick Tip

Rereading helps you understand the text better. If you read something, and you don't understand it, pause and reread. Look for details that help you understand the most important ideas.

> Page 127
>
> James was **motivated** to find a way to fly rockets. So, he went to college near his home for two years and then signed up for flight training at the United States Naval Academy. After four years at the academy, James joined the United States Navy and became a **professional** naval test pilot. His job was to fly planes before anyone else was allowed to fly them.

I read that James Lovell went to college and then to the United States Naval Academy. He signed up for flight training and became a professional naval test pilot. James Lovell became a pilot by going to school.

Your Turn Reread "Big Challenges" on page 128. How did the astronauts clean the air in their spacecraft?

_____

_____

_____

CHECK IN 1 2 3 4

Key Words and Photographs

"Rocketing into Space" is a **biography**. A biography

- is written by an author to tell the true story of a real person's life
- has the purpose of informing the reader
- includes text features, such as key words, photographs, and captions, to support the author's purpose

FIND TEXT EVIDENCE

I can tell that "Rocketing into Space" is a biography. It is the true story of James Lovell's life. The author uses key words and photographs with captions to better inform the reader.

Readers to Writers

Look at the photograph and read the caption on page 129. What do they tell you about an important event in James Lovell's life?

When you write a biography, consider using photographs and captions to support your purpose of informing the reader about important events in someone's life.

Page 128

Pilot to Astronaut

As a pilot, James spent more than half of his flying time in jets. He taught other pilots how to fly. He also worked as a **specialist** in air flight safety. Soon, the National Aeronautics and Space Administration, or NASA, put out a call for astronauts. James applied for the job because he had all the **essential** skills needed to fly into space. As a result, NASA chose him. By 1962, James Lovell was an astronaut! He had finally reached his goal.

Big Challenges

James flew on three space missions, and then in April 1970 he became **commander** of the Apollo 13 mission. This was a big responsibility and a great honor. This was also one of the biggest challenges of James's life.

Apollo 13 was supposed to land on the Moon. Two days

after leaving Earth, however, the **spacecraft** had a **serious** problem. One of its oxygen tanks exploded. The crew did not have enough power or air to breathe. They could not make it to the Moon.

James **communicated** with the experts at NASA. No one knew what to do at first. Then the team on the ground did some **research** and came up with a solution. The astronauts followed the team's directions and built an invention using plastic bags, cardboard, and tape. It worked! It cleaned the air in the spacecraft. But the next problem was even bigger. How were the astronauts going to get back to Earth?

NASA's team works to solve Apollo 13's problem.

Key Words
Key words are important words. They are in bold type.

Photographs
Photographs and their captions can show more about the events in the person's life.

Your Turn Find another key word in "Rocketing into Space." Why is this an important word in James Lovell's biography?

_____

_____

Central Idea and Relevant Details

The central idea is the author's most important point in a section of text. Relevant details are facts and information that are related to and support the central idea.

FIND TEXT EVIDENCE

I can reread page 127 and look for details that are relevant to the topic. If I think about what these details have in common, I can use them to figure out the central idea.

Central Idea James Lovell didn't let anything stop him from achieving his dream of becoming a pilot.
Detail James Lovell always dreamed of being a pilot.
Detail He planned to go to a special college, but he didn't have the money to attend.
Detail He attended the United States Naval Academy and became a professional naval test pilot.

Your Turn Reread "Pilot to Astronaut" on page 128. Record relevant details about how James Lovell became an astronaut in your graphic organizer. Use the details to figure out the central idea of the section.

CHECK IN 1 2 3 4

Central Idea

Detail

Detail

Detail

Respond to Reading

COLLABORATE Talk about the prompt below. Use your notes and evidence from the text to support your answer.

Why was having goals important to James Lovell's success?

_____

_____

_____

_____

_____

_____

_____

_____

_____

Quick Tip

Use these sentence starters to talk about James Lovell.

James Lovell was successful because . . .

His goals were important because . . .

Grammar Connections

As you write your response, check that you do not have any sentence fragments or run-ons. Each sentence should state a complete thought.

CHECK IN 1 2 3 4

National Heroes

COLLABORATE

The heroes we admire worked hard to achieve their goals. With a partner, think of national heroes you admire. They might be scientists, artists, athletes, or people who fought for the rights of others. Follow the research process to create a timeline that shows important events and accomplishments in that person's life.

James A. Lovell Jr. Meets His Goals		
1952	**1962**	**1970**
Completed training at US Naval Academy	Became an astronaut	Served as commander of the Apollo 13 space mission

Quick Tip

As you begin your research, some questions you may want to ask include: *When was my subject born? What are his or her most important accomplishments? What challenges did he or she face?*

Step 1 **Set a Goal** With a partner, choose a person to research.

Step 2 **Identify Sources** Think of questions to ask about your subject's life. Then find books and reliable websites to find information that can answer your questions.

Step 3 **Find and Record Information** Take notes on your sources. Remember to cite your sources.

Step 4 **Organize and Combine Information** Choose four or five events to include in your timeline. Put them in time order.

Step 5 **Create and Present** Create your timeline with your partner. Leave some space between each event to make your timeline easier to read. Use the timeline of James Lovell's life as a model. Share your work with the class.

CHECK IN 1 > 2 > 3 > 4

Looking Up to Ellen Ochoa

Literature Anthology: pages 462–471

? **How does the author use text features to help you understand Ellen Ochoa's biography?**

Talk About It Look at the text features on **Literature Anthology** pages 464 and 465. Discuss what you learned about Ellen Ochoa.

Cite Text Evidence What do the text features help you understand? Write text evidence in the chart.

 Make Inferences

Making an inference is using text evidence and what you know to make a conclusion about something not stated in a selection. Reread the second paragraph on page 464. Make an inference about the two people Ellen Ochoa looked up to.

Text Feature	What It Tells Me About Ellen Ochoa
quotation	
photo and caption, page 464	
photo and caption, page 465	

Write The author uses text features to help me understand

CHECK IN 1 2 3 4

How does the author use photographs and captions to help you understand that goals are important?

The main text says the "robotic arms work like human arms." How do the text features, such as photos and captions, help you understand how a robotic arm is like a human arm?

 Talk About It Reread the second paragraph on **Literature Anthology** page 464. Talk with a partner about Ellen's dream.

Cite Text Evidence What clues in the photographs and captions show how Ellen reached her goals? Write text evidence.

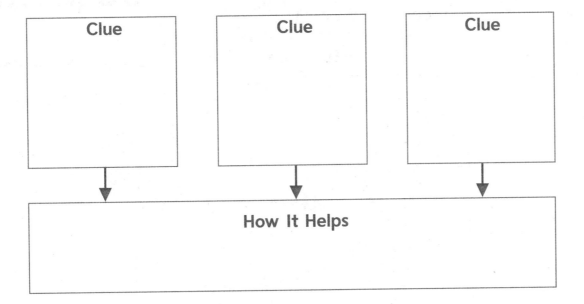

Clue	Clue	Clue

How It Helps

Write The author uses photographs and captions to help me

understand that goals are important by _____

_____

_____

_____

CHECK IN 1 2 3 4

? **Why is "Women Who Counted" a good heading for the sidebar?**

Talk About It Reread the sidebar on **Literature Anthology** page 470. Talk with a partner about what Dorothy Vaughan, Mary Jackson, and Katherine Johnson did at NASA.

Cite Text Evidence What details tell about the women at NASA and what they did? Write text evidence in the chart.

Text Evidence	Text Evidence	What I Understand

Write "Women Who Counted" is a good heading for the sidebar

because _____

_____

_____

_____

CHECK IN 1 2 3 4

Respond to Reading

COLLABORATE Talk about the prompt below. Use your notes and evidence from the text to support your answer.

Why do you think Ellen Ochoa was successful in reaching her goals?

_____

_____

_____

_____

_____

_____

_____

_____

Quick Tip

Use these sentence starters to talk about Ellen Ochoa.

Some of Ellen Ochoa's goals were . . .

Some things Ellen Ochoa did to reach her goals were . . .

Ellen Ochoa was successful because . . .

CHECK IN 1 ⟩ 2 ⟩ 3 ⟩ 4 ⟩

A Flight to Lunar City

1 Going to the Moon had been Maria's goal since she was five. The dream had motivated Maria to enter a science project in the National Space Contest. She had invented Robbie, the robot dog, as her science project. He was the perfect Moon pet. Maria and Robbie had won first prize —a trip to Lunar City, the first settlement on the Moon.

2 Now they were almost there! Robbie wriggled and squirmed. "Settle down!" Maria scolded. Sometimes Robbie was awfully wild, like a real puppy. Maria was thinking about adjusting his Personality Profile Program to make him a little calmer.

Literature Anthology:
pages 474–475

Reread and use the prompts to take notes in the text.

Underline words and phrases in paragraphs 1 and 2 that help you understand the setting of the story. Describe the setting here.

_____

_____

COLLABORATE

Talk with a partner about Maria's goal. **Circle** text evidence that tells how Maria achieved her goal. Summarize what she did.

_____

_____

_____

_____

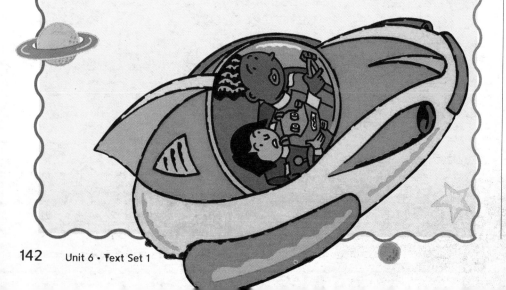

1   Just then Robbie jumped out of Maria's arms and leaped across the landing ship. He jumped onto the stick with all four paws and growled fiercely. He tugged and chewed on it. "Stop!" cried Maria.

2   All at once the control stick shifted into position. The lights came back on. The landing ship whooshed forward. "Robbie, you did it!" laughed Commander Buckley. "Good dog!" She handed Robbie back to Maria. "Now we can land on the Moon."

3   Maria smiled proudly. Robbie was the best robot dog ever!

Reread paragraph 1. **Underline** words and phrases that describe what Robbie does. **Circle** what Maria says.

COLLABORATE

Reread paragraphs 2 and 3. Talk with a partner about how Robbie solves the problem. **Draw a box around** details in the story that let you know how Commander Buckley and Maria feel. Describe how they feel on the lines below.

_____

_____

_____

_____

_____

_____

_____

_____

_____

How does the author use details to help you visualize how Robbie fixes the problem?

Talk About It Reread the excerpt on page 143. Talk with a partner about what Robbie does.

Cite Text Evidence What words and phrases show what Robbie does to fix the problem? Write text evidence in the chart.

Text Evidence	What I Visualize

Write I can visualize what Robbie does because the author

_____

_____

CHECK IN 1 2 3 4

Imagery

Writers use strong words and colorful details to create imagery. This helps readers form pictures in their minds as they read. Imagery helps readers better understand what is happening in a story.

FIND TEXT EVIDENCE

*In the last paragraph on page 474 in the **Literature Anthology,** the author of "A Flight to Lunar City" describes what happens to the lunar lander with phrases such as "jerked forward," "turned upside down," and "rolled sideways." The author uses strong words to create imagery and help the reader picture what is happening.*

> Suddenly there was a large bang. The lunar lander jerked forward and turned upside down. Then it rolled sideways.

Your Turn Reread paragraphs 1–4 on page 475.

- What are some other strong words and colorful details the author uses? _____

  _____

- How do the words and details you found add meaning to the text?

  _____

  _____

Readers to Writers

Help your readers picture what is happening in your story. When you write, choose a variety of strong and colorful words that show rather than tell what's happening. When readers visualize as they read, they can figure out and better understand the character's actions and feelings.

CHECK IN 1 > 2 > 3 > 4

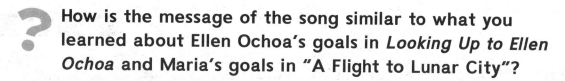

? **How is the message of the song similar to what you learned about Ellen Ochoa's goals in *Looking Up to Ellen Ochoa* and Maria's goals in "A Flight to Lunar City"?**

COLLABORATE

Talk About It Read the song lyrics. With a partner, talk about how you feel after reading it.

Cite Text Evidence **Underline** words and phrases in the lyrics that tell what the song's message is. Think about how the message makes you feel.

Write The message of this song is similar to what I

learned in the texts because _____

_____

_____

_____

_____

_____

_____

> **Quick Tip**
>
> Use the words in the lyrics to figure out the theme. This will help you compare the lyrics to the texts you read.

Turn Me 'Round

Ain't gonna let nobody
turn me 'round,
turn me 'round,
turn me 'round.
Ain't gonna let nobody
turn me 'round,
Keep on a-walkin',
keep on a-talkin',
Walkin' all over this land.

—African American
Spiritual

Design Pics/Bilderbuch

CHECK IN 〉 1 〉 2 〉 3 〉 4 〉

Write a Guide for Success

What did you learn about the importance of goals from the selections you read? What are some goals you have? How can you achieve those goals?

1. Look at your Build Knowledge notes in your reader's notebook.

2. Think of how the people you read about achieved their goals. What specific actions or qualities made them successful? Think of some tips or advice you could share with others to help them achieve goals they might have.

3. Create a short guide with tips that can help others achieve their goals. Your guide could be a booklet, pamphlet, or sheet of paper. Use examples from the texts you read. Include a personal example of your own, too.

4. At the end of your guide, add a sentence or two that explains why goals are important. Use new vocabulary words you've learned.

Think about what you learned in this text set. Fill in the bars on page 125.

Build Knowledge

Build Vocabulary

 Write new words you learned that are related to how we decide what's important. Draw lines and circles for the words you write.

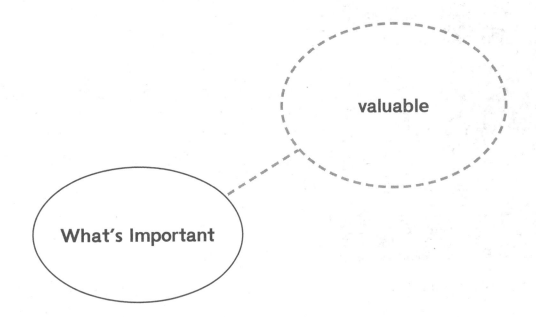

valuable

What's Important

 Go online to **my.mheducation.com** and read the "Snow Leopards" Blast. Think about why animals and their environments are important. Then blast back your response.

Think about what you already know. Fill in the bars. Keep doing your best!

Key

1 = I do not understand.

2 = I understand but need more practice.

3 = I understand.

4 = I understand and can teach someone.

What I Know Now

I can read and understand a drama and myth.

I can use text evidence to respond to a drama and myth.

I know how we decide what's important.

1 2 3 4

STOP You will come back to the next page later.

Think about what you learned. Fill in the bars. You can always improve, so keep trying!

What I Learned

I can read and understand a drama and myth.

1 > 2 > 3 > 4

I can use text evidence to respond to a drama and myth.

1 > 2 > 3 > 4

I know how we decide what's important.

1 > 2 > 3 > 4

My Goal I can read and understand a drama and myth.

TAKE NOTES

As you read, make note of interesting words and important events.

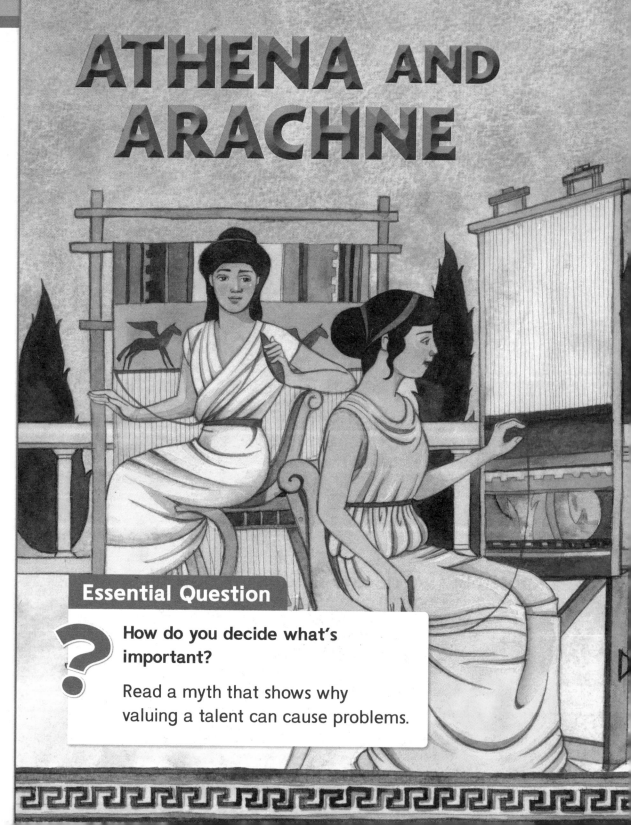

ATHENA AND ARACHNE

Essential Question

?

How do you decide what's important?

Read a myth that shows why valuing a talent can cause problems.

CHARACTERS

NARRATOR

ARACHNE: (uh-RAK-nee)

DIANA: Arachne's friend

ATHENA: a Greek goddess

MESSENGER

⟡ SCENE ONE ⟡

Athens, Greece, a long time ago, Arachne's home.

NARRATOR: Long ago, Arachne and her friend Diana sat weaving.

DIANA: Oh, Arachne! That cloth is so beautiful.

Arachne admires her cloth.

ARACHNE: I know. Many people want to **possess** my cloth, but few can afford it. Only those with great **wealth** can buy it.

DIANA: Yes, it's true that people value your cloth. It is one of their most valued possessions. Your weavings are a real **treasure.** Some say that you learned your weaving skill, or talent, from the goddess Athena.

ARACHNE: It was not **necessary** for me to learn from a goddess. I was born with my talent. I am a much better weaver than Athena, and I'm sure I could beat her in a weaving competition!

Diana is worried, stops weaving, and looks at Arachne.

DIANA: Ssshhh! I hope Athena isn't listening, or you're in big trouble!

ARACHNE: Nonsense! There's no reason to be **alarmed** or worried. Athena is much too busy to come down from Mount Olympus to compete with me.

Jenny Reynish

FIND TEXT EVIDENCE 🔍

Read

Scene One

Theme

Circle what Diana says to Arachne at the beginning of Scene One.

Stage Directions

Draw boxes around the stage directions in Scene One.

Make Predictions

Read Arachne's last line in Scene One. What prediction can you make about Athena?

_____

_____

_____

_____

Reread

Author's Craft

How does the author use dialogue to help you understand what Arachne is like?

FIND TEXT EVIDENCE

Read

Scene Two
Make Predictions

Check the prediction you made on page 153. **Circle** clues that tell whether you were correct.

Base Words

Draw a box around the word *apologize*. Write the base word.

_____

Scene Three
Dialogue

How does Athena trick Arachne?

_____

Underline text evidence.

Reread

Author's Craft

How does the author use stage directions to help you understand what the characters are doing?

⟶ SCENE TWO ⟵

Mount Olympus, home of Athena. A messenger arrives.

MESSENGER: Goddess Athena! I have news from Athens. The weaver Arachne says she can beat you in a weaving competition. She is **obsessed** with her skill and thinks she is the best weaver in Greece!

ATHENA: I'll show her who weaves the finest cloth! Her obsession with weaving must end. Please get me my cloak. *Messenger hands Athena her cloak.*

ATHENA: Arachne cannot talk about me that way! If she refuses to apologize, I will make her pay for her boastful words. Her **anguish** will be great!

⟶ SCENE THREE ⟵

Arachne's home. There is a knock at the door.

ARACHNE: Who's there?

ATHENA: Just an old woman with a question.

Athena is hiding under her cloak. She enters the room.

ATHENA: Is it true that you challenged the goddess Athena to a weaving competition?

ARACHNE: Yes, that's right. *Athena drops her cloak.*

ATHENA: Well, I am Athena. I am here to compete with you!

DIANA: Arachne, please don't! It is unwise to compete with a goddess!

Arachne and Athena sit down at the empty looms and begin to weave furiously.

ARACHNE: I am ready to win and get my reward!

ATHENA: There's no prize if you lose!

NARRATOR: Arachne and Athena both wove beautiful cloths. However, Arachne's cloth was filled with pictures of the gods being unkind.

ATHENA: Arachne, your weaving is beautiful, but I am insulted and upset by the pictures you chose to weave. You are boastful, and your cloth is mean and unkind. For that, I will punish you.

Athena points dramatically at Arachne. Arachne falls behind her loom and crawls out as a spider.

ATHENA: Arachne, you will spend the rest of your life weaving and living in your own web.

NARRATOR: Arachne was mean and boastful, so Athena turned her into a spider. That's why spiders are now called arachnids. Arachne learned that bragging and too much pride can lead to trouble.

⇒ **THE END** ⇐

Summarize

Review your notes on "Athena and Arachne." Summarize the text using the theme and plot events.

FIND TEXT EVIDENCE

Read

Scene Three

Theme

How does Arachne react to Athena's challenge?

_____

_____

Underline text evidence.

Dialogue

Why is Athena insulted and upset by Arachne's weaving?

_____

_____

Circle text evidence.

Reread

Author's Craft

How does the author help you understand how something came to be?

Vocabulary

Use the sentences to talk with a partner about each word. Then answer the questions.

alarmed

Jess was **alarmed** as she saw her basketball bounce over the fence.

Describe how you would look if you were alarmed by something.

_____

_____

anguish

Andy felt **anguish** when he realized his bike was missing.

What is another word that means the same as *anguish*?

_____

_____

necessary

Food is **necessary** for all living things.

What other things are necessary for living things?

_____

_____

obsessed

Victor is **obsessed** with space and is saving for a telescope.

Name something you are obsessed with.

_____

_____

possess

Dan and Meg **possess** a huge bunch of colorful pencils.

Tell about something you possess.

_____

_____

Build Your Word List Look back at the list of interesting words you noted on page 152. In your reader's notebook, draw a word web and write more forms of one of the words. Use an online or print dictionary to help you.

reward

Mom made my favorite dinner as a **reward** for passing my math test.

What reward would you like to get?

_____

_____

treasure

Lila found a real **treasure** at the book sale.

Tell about a treasure you have.

_____

_____

wealth

We are counting our coins to see how much **wealth** we have.

What is another word for _wealth_?

_____

_____

_____

Base Words

A base word is the simplest form of a word. It can help you figure out the meaning of a related word.

🔍 FIND TEXT EVIDENCE

In "Athena and Arachne," I see the word competition. _I think the base word of_ competition _is_ compete. _I know_ compete _means "to try to win." I think a_ competition _is "a contest where people try to win."_

I am a much better weaver than Athena, and I'm sure I could beat her in a weaving competition!

Your Turn Find the base word in the word below. Then use it to figure out the meaning of the word.

possessions, page 153 _____

_____

_____

CHECK IN 〉 1 〉 2 〉 3 〉 4 〉

Make Predictions

Use details in the story to predict what will happen next. Read on to confirm, or check it. Correct your prediction if it is not right.

Quick Tip

Look at the stage directions and dialogue to help you correct or confirm your prediction.

🔍 FIND TEXT EVIDENCE

You may have made a prediction about Arachne. What clues on page 153 helped you guess what would happen?

> Page 153
>
> **DIANA:** Oh, Arachne! That cloth is so beautiful.
>
> *Arachne admires her cloth.*
>
> **ARACHNE:** I know. Many people want to **possess** my cloth, but few can afford it. Only those with great **wealth** can buy it.
>
> **DIANA:** Yes, it's true that people value your cloth. It is one of their most valued possessions. Your weavings are a real **treasure.** Some say that you learned your weaving skill, or talent, from the goddess Athena.
>
> **ARACHNE:** It was not **necessary** for me to learn from a goddess. I was born with my talent. I am a much better weaver than Athena, and I'm sure I could beat her in a weaving competition!

I predicted that Arachne and Athena would compete. I read that <u>Arachne says she is a better weaver than Athena and could beat her in a contest.</u> *I read on to confirm, or check my prediction.*

 Your Turn What did you predict would happen when Athena went to see Arachne? Write your prediction and the text evidence that supports it or changes it.

Elements of a Play

"Athena and Arachne" is a **myth** and a **drama**, or play. A myth tells how something came to be. A drama

- is a story that is performed on a stage
- has elements such as dialogue, stage directions, acts, and scenes

FIND TEXT EVIDENCE

I see that "Athena and Arachne" is a myth and a play. It is divided into three scenes. The play uses dialogue and stage directions to tell how spiders came to weave webs.

Page 154

⟪⟫⟪⟫⟪⟫⟪⟫⟪⟫⟪⟫⟪⟫⟪⟫⟪⟫⟪⟫⟪⟫⟪⟫⟪⟫⟪⟫

⟫ SCENE TWO ⟪

Mount Olympus, home of Athena. A messenger arrives.

MESSENGER: Goddess Athena! I have news from Athens. The weaver Arachne says she can beat you in a weaving competition. She is **obsessed** with her skill and thinks she is the best weaver in Greece!

ATHENA: I'll show her who weaves the finest cloth! Her obsession with weaving must end. Please get me my cloak. *Messenger hands Athena her cloak.*

ATHENA: Arachne cannot talk about me that way! If she refuses to apologize, I will make her pay for her boastful words. Her **anguish** will be great!

⟫ SCENE THREE ⟪

Arachne's home. There is a knock at the door.

ARACHNE: Who's there?

ATHENA: Just an old woman with a question. *Athena is hiding under her cloak. She enters the room.*

ATHENA: Is it true that you challenged the goddess Athena to a weaving competition?

ARACHNE: Yes, that's right. *Athena drops her cloak.*

ATHENA: Well, I am Athena. I am here to compete with you!

DIANA: Arachne, please don't! It is unwise to compete with a goddess!

Arachne and Athena sit down at the empty looms and begin

Scenes

A scene is a division, or part, of a play.

Stage Directions

Stage directions tell what the characters do and how they move. They also share information about the setting.

Dialogue

Dialogue is the words the characters speak. It can reveal the characters' perspectives, or thoughts and feelings.

Your Turn How does Diana's dialogue on page 154 show her character's perspective?

COLLABORATE

_____

_____

Readers to Writers

An act is a group of scenes in a drama. Writers use the act to tell big parts of the story, such as the beginning, middle, and end. When you write a play, think about how your acts and scenes work together to tell the whole story.

CHECK IN 1 2 3 4

Theme

The theme of a story is the author's message. Authors develop the theme with details, such as information about what the characters do and say. Pay attention to details to infer, or figure out, the theme.

Quick Tip

To tell the difference between theme and topic, remember that theme is the author's message and topic is the subject of the story. The topic of "Athena and Arachne" is a weaving contest.

🔍 FIND TEXT EVIDENCE

In "Athena and Arachne," Arachne is very proud of her cloth. She even says her weaving is better than the goddess Athena's. I can use these details and more to help me infer, or figure out, the theme.

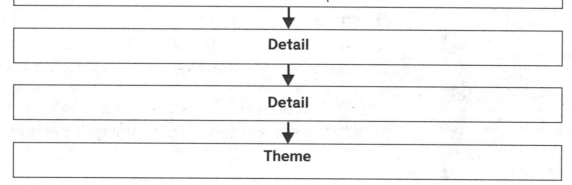

Detail
Arachne says that many people want to possess her cloth, but few can afford it. Only those with great wealth can buy it.

↓

Detail
Arachne says she is a better weaver than Athena and could beat her in a competition.

↓

Detail

↓

Detail

↓

Theme

Your Turn Reread "Athena and Arachne." List more important details from "Athena and Arachne" in the graphic organizer. Then use the details to figure out the theme of the myth.

CHECK IN 1 2 3 4

Detail

Arachne says that many people want to possess her cloth, but few can afford it. Only those with great wealth can buy it.

↓

Detail

Arachne says she is a better weaver than Athena and could beat her in a competition.

↓

Detail

↓

Detail

↓

Theme

Respond to Reading

Talk about the prompt below. Use your notes and evidence from the text to support your answer.

Why do you think myths, such as "Athena and Arachne," were created by the ancient Greeks?

_____

_____

_____

_____

_____

_____

_____

_____

_____

_____

Quick Tip

Use these sentence starters to talk about myths.

In "Athena and Arachne," I read . . .

Ancient Greeks may have created myths like this because . . .

Grammar Connections

As you write your response, be sure to check that you are putting quotation marks at the beginning and at the end of the exact words a person says. Use commas to set off a direct quotation.

For example, "Oh, Arachne!" said Diana. "That cloth is so beautiful."

CHECK IN 1 2 3 4

What We Think Is Important

COLLABORATE

Much of what we think is important is what other people think is important, too. Follow the research process to gather information from others about something you think is important. Then create a bar graph to show what you have learned.

Step 1 **Set a Goal** With a partner, brainstorm a list of things you think are important. Select one and write it here.

_____

Step 2 **Identify Sources** Think of a question that is related to your topic and has at least four possible answers. Then choose six classmates who can answer your question.

Step 3 **Find and Record Information** Ask your six classmates your question. Write down which answers they choose.

Step 4 **Organize and Combine Information** Organize your classmates' answers by counting how many times each answer was chosen.

Step 5 **Create and Present** Create your bar graph. Write the answers to your question along the bottom. Add a title. Fill in your graph with the answers you collected. Use the bar graph on this page as a model. Share your graph with the class.

Quick Tip

Think about what's important to you and your classmates. Is it taking care of your pets? Spending time with friends and family? Eating healthful snacks? Pick one topic and find out what others think is important.

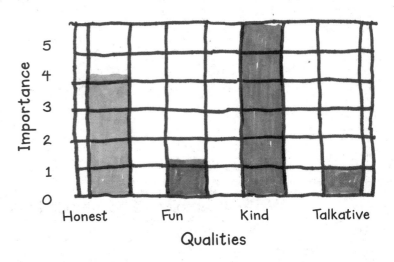

Qualities of a Good Friend

CHECK IN 1 2 3 4

King Midas and the Golden Touch

 How does the author help you visualize how much King Midas loves gold?

Literature Anthology: pages 476–489

 Talk About It Reread **Literature Anthology** pages 478 and 479. With a partner, talk about what King Midas does.

Cite Text Evidence What words, phrases, and images help to show how King Midas feels about gold? Write text evidence in the web.

Synthesize Information

Look for text evidence that shows characters' words and actions. Then draw a conclusion about how much King Midas loves gold.

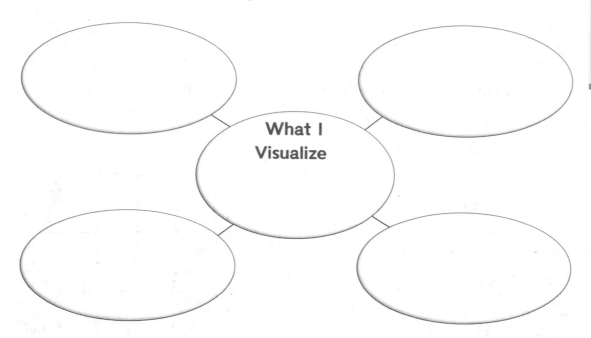

What I Visualize

Write I can picture how much Midas loves gold because the author

_____

_____

CHECK IN   1   2   3   4

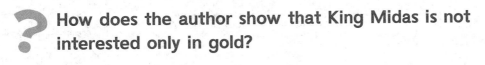 **How does the author show that King Midas is not interested only in gold?**

 Talk About It Reread **Literature Anthology** pages 482 and 483. Talk with a partner about King Midas's words and actions.

Cite Text Evidence What clues help you learn more about King Midas's character, or traits and qualities? Record text evidence.

Clue

Clue

Clue

What It Shows

Write The author helps me understand King Midas's character by

_____

_____

Quick Tip

Use these sentence starters to talk about King Midas.

The author describes how King Midas . . .

This tells me that he feels . . .

 ### Evaluate Information

Read the text carefully to look for evidence that shows King Midas's words and actions. Think about what the evidence tells you about the kind of person King Midas is.

CHECK IN 〉1〉2〉3〉4〉

? **How does the author show that something might happen to Marigold later in the story?**

COLLABORATE

Talk About It Reread **Literature Anthology** pages 484 and 485. Talk with a partner about what happens to the stone and the rose.

Cite Text Evidence What clues show that something might happen to Marigold? Write text evidence.

Make Inferences

Think about what you already know and the author's words and phrases. Then make an inference about what might happen between Marigold and her father later in the story.

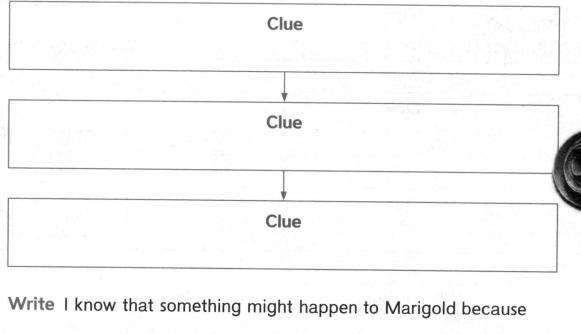

Clue

↓

Clue

↓

Clue

Write I know that something might happen to Marigold because

_____

_____

_____

_____

CHECK IN 1 2 3 4

Illustration: Gail Armstrong

Respond to Reading

Talk about the prompt below. Use your notes and evidence from the text to support your answer.

Why does the traveler teach King Midas a lesson?

_____

_____

_____

_____

_____

_____

_____

_____

_____

_____

_____

Quick Tip

Use these sentence starters to talk about King Midas.

I read that King Midas . . .

When he meets the traveler, he . . .

The traveler teaches King Midas a lesson because . . .

CHECK IN 1 2 3 4

Carlos's Gift

Literature Anthology:
pages 492–495

1   Carlos wanted a puppy in the worst way. He dreamed about puppies—big ones, little ones, spotted ones, frisky ones. Now it was his birthday, and Carlos had one thing on his mind. A puppy! When Mama handed him a flat, square box, Carlos almost started to cry.

2   It was a book about caring for dogs.

3   Papa smiled, "You need to learn how to care for a puppy before you get one."

4   Carlos read the book that night. He found a photograph of the exact kind of bulldog puppy that he craved. He eagerly showed Mama the next morning.

Reread and use the prompts to take notes in the text.

Underline phrases in paragraph 1 that show how much Carlos wants a puppy. **Circle** clues that show how he feels when Mama gives him his present. Summarize Carlos's feelings.

_____

_____

_____

COLLABORATE

Reread paragraph 4. Talk with a partner about what Carlos does. **Draw a box around** two phrases that show how Carlos feels about learning to care for a dog.

1   Carlos started working at the shelter on Saturday. His assignment was sweeping. Afterwards, the dogs scampered out to play. One dog named Pepper had a funny curly tail that never stopped wagging. She was fully grown but as playful as a puppy. When Pepper leaped in the pile of sticks and leaves that Carlos had just swept up, he laughed.

2   Carlos went to the shelter every weekend. He began to treasure his time with the dogs, especially Pepper. One day Carlos asked why Pepper was still at the shelter.

3   Miss Jones sighed, "We've had trouble finding a home for Pepper. Most people don't want such an energetic dog."

4   Carlos suddenly realized he didn't want a bulldog puppy. He wanted Pepper. "I wish I could buy her," he replied.

In paragraph 1, **draw a box around** words and phrases that describe Pepper. **Underline** the text evidence in paragraph 3 that tells why Pepper has not found a home. Summarize why.

_____

_____

COLLABORATE

Talk with a partner about what Miss Jones and Carlos say about Pepper. **Circle** text evidence to support your discussion.

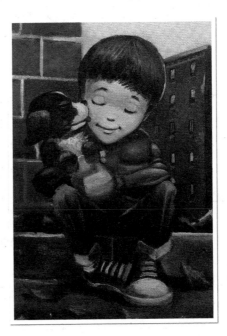

How does the author use dialogue to show how Carlos feels about Pepper?

Make Inferences

Read the dialogue carefully to make an inference about how Carlos feels.

Talk About It Reread paragraphs 2–4 on page 169. Talk with a partner about how Carlos reacts to what Miss Jones says.

Cite Text Evidence What does Carlos think and say about Pepper? What does Miss Jones say? Write text evidence in the chart.

Text Evidence	How Carlos Feels

Write I know how Carlos feels about Pepper because the author uses

dialogue to _____

_____

CHECK IN 1 2 3 4

Plot: Character Development

Authors of fiction develop their characters throughout a story. This means they show how the characters change from the beginning to the end. Authors show this change by including details about how the characters think, feel, and respond to situations, or events.

FIND TEXT EVIDENCE

*In paragraphs 1–3 on page 492 of "Carlos's Gift" in the **Literature Anthology,** the author shows how disappointed Carlos is when he doesn't receive a puppy for his birthday. The author also reveals that Carlos needs to learn about taking care of a puppy.*

> When Mama handed him a flat, square box, Carlos almost started to cry.
>
> It was a book about caring for dogs.
>
> Papa smiled, "You need to learn how to care for a puppy before you get one."

Your Turn Reread the ending of "Carlos's Gift" on page 495.

- How does the author show that Carlos has developed?

_____

_____

_____

Readers to Writers

Fiction is more interesting when characters change and learn new things throughout a story. When you write your own fiction stories, think about how you can include details about your characters' thoughts, feelings, and actions to show their development.

CHECK IN 1 2 3 4

? **How does the photographer of the picture below show what is important? How is this like what the authors do in *King Midas and the Golden Touch* and "Carlos's Gift"?**

Quick Tip

You can tell what someone thinks is important by looking at their actions. Look at what Chloe is doing to understand what she thinks is important.

Talk About It Look at the photograph and read the caption. Talk with a partner about what you see happening in the photograph.

Cite Text Evidence Circle clues that show how Chloe is helping. **Underline** the words in the caption that tell what Chloe is doing. **Draw a box around** the part of the photograph that helps you know how Chloe feels.

Write The photographer and authors show

what's important by _____

_____

_____

_____

_____

_____

Chloe is always busy, but she volunteers at the food bank every week.

CHECK IN 1 ⟩ 2 ⟩ 3 ⟩ 4 ⟩

My Goal I know how we decide what's important.

Draw a Comic Strip

Think about what you have learned from the selections this week. What have they taught you about how we decide what is important? What can we learn from understanding more about the things that are important to us?

1. Look at your Build Knowledge notes in your reader's notebook.

2. Choose three characters from the selections you read. Think about the treasures or items the characters value, or think are important.

3. Create a comic strip with four boxes. In the first three boxes, draw the characters and treasures you chose from the selections. In the final box, draw yourself and your own treasure, or something that is important to you.

4. Below your comic strip, write a couple of sentences that explain what you can learn about people by understanding the things they value. Use new vocabulary words in your writing.

Think about what you learned in this text set. Fill in the bars on page 151.

Build Vocabulary

 Write new words you learned about what makes us laugh.
Draw lines and circles for the words you write.

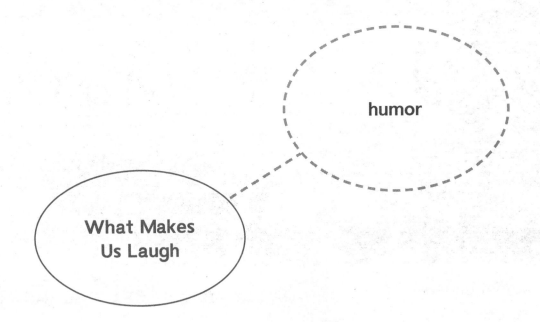

humor

What Makes
Us Laugh

 Go online to **my.mheducation.com** and read the Blast titled
"The Best Medicine." Think about what scientists can learn by
studying what makes us laugh. Then blast back your response.

Think about what you already know. Fill in the bars. We all do better with practice.

What I Know Now

Key	
1 =	I do not understand.
2 =	I understand but need more practice.
3 =	I understand.
4 =	I understand and can teach someone.

I can read and understand poetry.

1 › 2 › 3 › 4 ›

I can use text evidence to respond to poetry.

1 › 2 › 3 › 4 ›

I know what makes us laugh.

1 › 2 › 3 › 4 ›

 **STOP** You will come back to the next page later.

Think about what you learned. Fill in the bars. Good job!

What I Learned

I can read and understand poetry.

1 2 3 4

I can use text evidence to respond to poetry.

1 2 3 4

I know what makes us laugh.

1 2 3 4

My Goal

I can read and understand poetry.

TAKE NOTES

As you read, make note of interesting words and details.

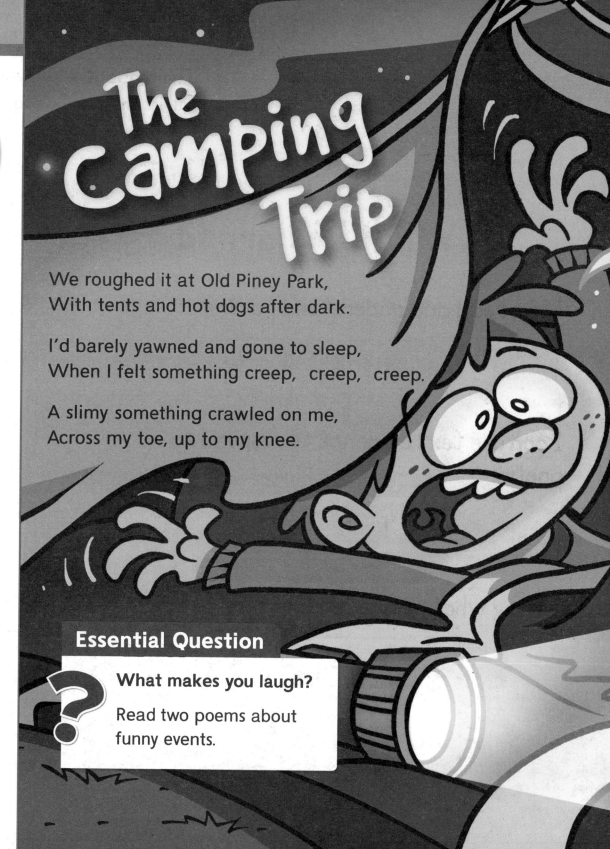

The Camping Trip

We roughed it at Old Piney Park,
With tents and hot dogs after dark.

I'd barely yawned and gone to sleep,
When I felt something creep, creep, creep.

A slimy something crawled on me,
Across my toe, up to my knee.

Essential Question

What makes you laugh?

Read two poems about funny events.

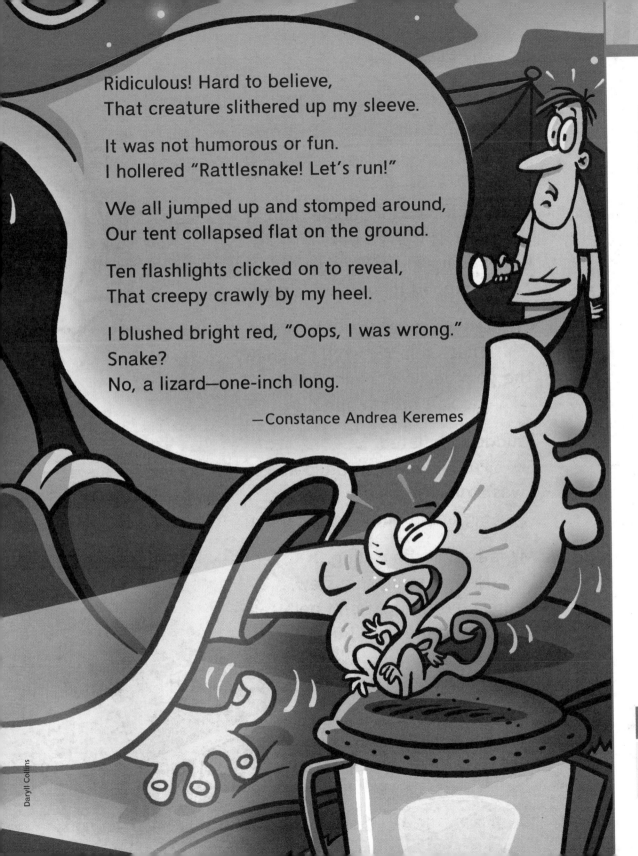

Ridiculous! Hard to believe,
That creature slithered up my sleeve.

It was not humorous or fun.
I hollered "Rattlesnake! Let's run!"

We all jumped up and stomped around,
Our tent collapsed flat on the ground.

Ten flashlights clicked on to reveal,
That creepy crawly by my heel.

I blushed bright red, "Oops, I was wrong."
Snake?
No, a lizard—one-inch long.

—Constance Andrea Keremes

Daryll Collins

FIND TEXT EVIDENCE

Read

Page 178

Stanzas
How many lines does the first stanza have?

Rhymed Verse
Circle words that rhyme in the second stanza. What two words rhyme in the third stanza?

Page 179

Character Perspective
How does the speaker feel when he finds out what was crawling on him?

Underline text evidence.

Reread

Author's Craft

How does the poet help you see how the speaker feels?

FIND TEXT EVIDENCE

Read

Page 180

Character Perspective

How does the speaker feel about bubble gum?

_____

_____

_____

Circle the text evidence.

Idioms

Underline two idioms in the fourth stanza. What do the idioms mean?

_____

_____

_____

Reread

Author's Craft

How does the poet help you understand what _inflated_ means?

Bubble Gum

I bought a pack of bubble gum,
    As I do every week,
Unwrapping 10 or 20 sticks,
    I popped them in my cheek.

I started masticating,
    That's a fancy word for chew,
The gum became a juicy gob,
    I took a breath and blew.

I suddenly inflated,
    Puffing up like a balloon,
I was a giant bubble,
    Big and round as a full moon.

My father hit the ceiling,
    He was really in a stew,
He hollered, "Stop! Don't go!"
    As out the door I flew.

The neighbors' eyes were popping.
    They dropped everything to see.
I was the entertainment of the day.
    Forget about TV.

If you like bubble gum, beware—
    Chew just one stick a day,
Or you'll become a bubble, too
And float up Up AWAY!

I saw my friends below me,
    And let loose a mighty roar.
WHOOSH!
All my air blew out,
    And I was just a kid once more.

— Diana Kent

Daryll Collins

Make Connections

Which poem has the funniest events
or characters?

FIND TEXT EVIDENCE

Read

Page 181

Character Perspective

How do the neighbors feel about
the speaker's adventure?

_____

_____

_____

Circle text evidence.

Events

What happens to the speaker at
the end of the poem?

_____

_____

Underline text evidence.

Reread

Author's Craft

How does the poet help you
understand how the speaker
feels at the end of the poem?

Vocabulary

Use the sentences to talk with a partner about each word. Then answer the questions.

entertainment

Grandpa and Devon think playing chess is great **entertainment**.

What do you like to do for entertainment?

_____

_____

humorous

Evan laughed at Nick's **humorous** story.

Describe a humorous time when you laughed.

_____

_____

ridiculous

Jess wore a **ridiculous** clown nose and made his friends giggle.

What's another word for *ridiculous*?

_____

_____

slithered

The long, thin snake **slithered** across the floor.

What does *slithered* mean?

_____

_____

Poetry Words

narrative poem

My favorite **narrative poem** tells about Paul Revere's ride.

What story would you tell in a narrative poem?

_____

_____

rhyme

The words *moon* and *spoon* **rhyme** because they end in the same sound.

Write two words that rhyme with *moon* and *spoon*.

_____

_____

rhythm

Ben's poem has a **rhythm** that sounds like a drumbeat.

Why might a poet include rhythm in a poem?

_____

_____

stanza

Each **stanza** in Maggie's poem has five lines.

How can you tell how many stanzas a poem has?

_____

_____

Build Your Word List Reread the fourth stanza on page 179. Draw a box around the word *reveal*. In your reader's notebook, make a list of synonyms and a list of antonyms for *reveal*. Use a thesaurus to help you add to each list.

Idioms

An idiom is a phrase with a figurative meaning. This means it doesn't mean what it literally says. The phrase "raining cats and dogs" is an idiom. It doesn't mean that cats and dogs are actually falling from the sky. It means it's raining very hard.

FIND TEXT EVIDENCE

On page 178 of "The Camping Trip," the phrase "roughed it" is an idiom. I can use clues to figure out that "roughed it" means "to live without the usual comforts of home."

We roughed it at Old Piney Park,
With tents and hot dogs after dark.

Your Turn Figure out the meaning of the idiom.

eyes were popping, page 181

_____

_____

CHECK IN 1 2 3 4

LITERARY ELEMENTS

Rhythm and Rhymed Verse

Rhythm is the pattern of stressed, or emphasized, and unstressed syllables in a poem. **Rhymed verse** is a form of poetry that uses rhyme. In rhymed verse, words that appear at the end of two or more lines in the poem end in the same sound. Poets use rhythm and rhyme to give their poems a musical quality.

 FIND TEXT EVIDENCE

Read aloud "Bubble Gum" on pages 180 and 181. Listen for words that rhyme. Clap your hands as you read to follow the poem's rhythm.

Quick Tip

Read poems aloud slowly and clap for each syllable to listen for the rhythm. Listen for rhymes at the end of lines. Remember that the same sound can have different spellings, as in *flew* and *blue*.

Page 180

I bought a pack of bubble gum,
    As I do every week,
Unwrapping 10 or 20 sticks,
    I popped them in my cheek.

I started masticating,
    That's a fancy word for chew,
The gum became a juicy gob,
    I took a breath and blew.

In the second and fourth lines, the words week *and* cheek *rhyme. I noticed other rhyming words in the second and fourth lines of the other stanzas. This pattern of rhyme creates a rhythm in the poem.*

 Your Turn Reread "The Camping Trip" on pages 178 and 179. Find more examples of rhythm and rhyme and record them below.

_____

_____

_____

CHECK IN 1 > 2 > 3 > 4 >

Stanzas and Events

Narrative poetry is a form of poetry that tells a story. It includes plot events, characters, and a setting. A narrative poem is usually broken into different **stanzas**, or groups of lines. A narrative poem can have any number of lines or stanzas. It often features rhythm and rhyme.

FIND TEXT EVIDENCE

I can tell that "Bubble Gum" is a narrative poem. It tells a story with a character, setting, and plot events. It is broken up into seven stanzas. It features rhythm and rhyme.

Readers to Writers

Look at the series of events in "Bubble Gum." What happens at the beginning of the poem? What happens at the end? When you write a narrative poem, think about the events to include in the beginning, middle, and end.

Page 180

Bubble Gum

I bought a pack of bubble gum,
     As I do every week,
Unwrapping 10 or 20 sticks,
     I popped them in my cheek.

I started masticating,
     That's a fancy word for chew,
The gum became a juicy gob,
     I took a breath and blew.

I suddenly inflated,
     Puffing up like a balloon,
I was a giant bubble,
     Big and round as a full moon.

My father hit the ceiling,
     He was really in a stew,
He hollered, "Stop! Don't go!"
     As out the door I flew.

A stanza is a group of lines in a poem. On this page, there are four stanzas of four lines each.

"Bubble Gum" tells a humorous story. Each stanza tells about an event.

COLLABORATE

Your Turn Reread "The Camping Trip" on pages 178 and 179. Explain why it is a narrative poem. Tell how many stanzas there are.

_____

_____

_____

CHECK IN 1 2 3 4

Character Perspective

Character perspective refers to what a character thinks and feels about someone or something. Narrative poetry may share the perspectives of the speaker and other characters in the poem. Look for details that reveal a character's thoughts and feelings to understand his or her perspective.

 FIND TEXT EVIDENCE

In "The Camping Trip," the speaker feels something crawling on him. Details the speaker shares can help me understand his perspective.

Details
A slimy something crawled on me

↓

Perspective

 Your Turn Reread "The Camping Trip." Find more details about how the speaker feels about the creepy creature. Write them in the graphic organizer. Use the details to find his perspective.

CHECK IN 1 2 3 4

Daryll Collins

Details

Perspective

Respond to Reading

COLLABORATE Talk about the prompt below. Use your notes and evidence from the text to support your answer.

Why do you think the poems you read are funny?

_____

_____

_____

_____

_____

_____

_____

_____

_____

_____

Quick Tip

Use these sentence starters to talk about the poems.

"The Camping Trip" is funny because . . .

"Bubble Gum" is funny because . . .

Grammar Connections

As you write your response, be sure to put direct quotes from the poem in quotation marks.

CHECK IN 1 2 3 4

Tall Tales

Tall tales are stories with larger-than-life characters. They tell about events that could not really happen. They use hyperbole, or exaggeration, to entertain readers and make them laugh. With a partner, follow the research process to learn more about a character in a tall tale. Make a poster to show what you learned.

Step 1 **Set a Goal** Brainstorm a list of characters in tall tales. You can use books, websites, or your teacher for help. Choose one character to learn more about.

Step 2 **Identify Sources** Use books and websites to learn more about the character you chose. Think of some questions you can answer with research. You might ask: *What are some of the things the character is known for? What qualities or features does he or she have? What larger-than-life actions is the character able to do?*

Step 3 **Find and Record Information** Use your sources to answer your questions. Take notes and cite your sources.

Step 4 **Organize and Combine Information** Plan your poster. What information about your character do you want to share? Think of some illustrations you can include.

Step 5 **Create and Present** Complete your poster. Include information about your character that you learned from your sources. Use illustrations to make your poster colorful and interesting.

Quick Tip

Johnny Appleseed, Paul Bunyan, Pecos Bill, and Windy Gale are a few examples of heroes in tall tales. You can read about Windy Gale in "Windy Gale and the Great Hurricane" on pages 434 and 435 in the **Literature Anthology**.

CHECK IN 〉 1 〉 2 〉 3 〉 4 〉

Ollie's Escape

Literature Anthology: pages 496–498

? How does the poet use words and phrases to make the poem funny?

Talk About It Reread **Literature Anthology** page 497. Look at the illustration. Talk with a partner about what makes this poem funny.

Cite Text Evidence What words and phrases make the poem funny? Write text evidence in the chart.

Make Inferences

What inference can you make about the meaning of *squiggled* as it is used in the poem?

Text Evidence	Why It's Funny

Write The poet uses words and phrases to make the poem funny by

_____

_____

CHECK IN 1 2 3 4

How does the poet use idioms to help you visualize the characters' actions?

Talk About It Reread **Literature Anthology** pages 497 and 498. Talk about what Principal Poole does when he sees Ollie.

Cite Text Evidence What words and phrases help you visualize the characters' actions? Write text evidence in the chart.

Idiom	What I Visualize

Write The author uses idioms to describe the characters' actions to

_____

_____

_____

My Goal I can use text evidence to respond to poetry.

Respond to Reading

COLLABORATE Talk about the prompt below. Use your notes and evidence from the text to support your answer.

Why do you think "Ollie's Escape" is funny?

Quick Tip

Use these sentence starters to talk about "Ollie's Escape."

One thing that is funny in "Ollie's Escape" is . . .

Another funny thing that happens is . . .

CHECK IN 1 > 2 > 3 > 4

The Gentleman Bookworm

Literature Anthology:
pages 500–501

? How does the illustration help you understand the details in the poem?

COLLABORATE

Talk About It Look at the illustration on **Literature Anthology** pages 500 and 501. Talk about what the bookworms are doing.

Cite Text Evidence What clues in the illustration help you understand what the bookworms are doing? Write them in the chart. Explain what the clues help you understand.

Illustration Clues	→	What I Understand

Synthesize Information

Use the illustration to help you understand the title of the poem. Look closely at the details about the main character and what he does to understand why the speaker of the poem calls him a gentleman.

Write The poet uses the illustration to _____

_____

_____

CHECK IN ⟩ 1 ⟩ 2 ⟩ 3 ⟩ 4 ⟩

How does the poet use personification to help you visualize what the bookworms are doing?

Talk About It Reread **Literature Anthology** page 501. Talk with a partner about what the bookworms are doing that people usually do.

Cite Text Evidence What words and phrases describe things that people do? Write text evidence and say what you visualize.

Quick Tip

Take turns reading the poem aloud with a partner as the other acts out what the poem says. Miming the actions will help you visualize what the text is describing.

Text Evidence	What I Visualize

Write The poet uses personification in the poem by _____

_____

_____

_____

CHECK IN 1 2 3 4

Figurative Language

Authors can make their writing more interesting and humorous by using figurative language. A common form of figurative language in poetry is alliteration. This is when a series of words begin with the same sound, as in *wild, whistling wind*. Another common form of figurative language is personification. This is giving human features or behaviors to something nonhuman, as in *the Sun smiled upon me*.

 FIND TEXT EVIDENCE

*On page 501 of "The Gentleman Bookworm" in the **Literature Anthology**, I see the phrase "worm, wiggling." This is an example of alliteration. The worm then asks the host when they will eat. The worm speaking like a human is an example of personification.*

> A worm, wiggling up to the host,
>   Said, "When do we eat?"

 Your Turn Reread "The Gentleman Bookworm."

- What is another example of alliteration?

  _____

- What is another example personification?

  _____

  _____

Readers to Writers

There are many forms of figurative language. Similes, metaphors, and hyperbole are other examples. Think of how you can use figurative language in your own writing to make it more creative and interesting to read.

CHECK IN   1   2   3   4

? How is the way poet Henry Leigh makes you feel similar to how the poets of "Ollie's Escape" and "The Gentleman Bookworm" make you feel?

COLLABORATE **Talk About It** Read the excerpt from "The Twins." Talk with a partner about what is funny about the poem.

Cite Text Evidence **Circle** the words in the poem that rhyme. **Underline** phrases that are funny. Think about the tone, or feeling, of the poem. How is it similar to the tone of the other poems you read?

Write All three poets _____

_____

_____

_____

> From
> # "The Twins"
>
> In form and feature, face and limb,
>   I grew so like my brother,
> That folks got taking me for him,
>   And each for one another.
> It puzzled all our kith and kin,
>   It reach'd an awful pitch;
> For one of us was born a twin,
>   Yet not a soul knew which.
> One day (to make the matter worse),
>   Before our names were fix'd,
> As we were being wash'd by nurse
>   We got completely mix'd.
>
> — Henry Leigh

CHECK IN   1   2   3   4

My Goal I know what makes us laugh.

Write a Top 5 List

Think about the humorous, or funny, poems you read. What have you learned about what makes us laugh? Why do you think laughter and humor is important?

1 Look at your Build Knowledge notes in your reader's notebook.

2 Think about some of the things you found funny in the poems you read. Also think of other things that have made you laugh. Choose five things and rank them from one to five. Number one should be the one you thought was funniest.

3 Next to each item in your list, write a sentence that tells why you thought it was funny. Use new vocabulary words in your writing.

Think about what you learned in this text set. Fill in the bars on page 177.

Think about what you already know. Fill in the bars. Now let's get started!

Key

1 = I do not understand.

2 = I understand but need more practice.

3 = I understand.

4 = I understand and can teach someone.

What I Know Now

I can write an expository essay.

I can synthesize information from three sources.

| 1 | 2 | 3 | 4 |

STOP You will come back to the next page later.

Think about what you learned. Fill in the bars. The more you write, the more you'll improve.

What I Learned

I can write an expository essay.

1 2 3 4

I can synthesize information from three sources.

1 2 3 4

WRITING

WRITE TO SOURCES

You will answer an expository writing prompt using sources and a rubric.

ANALYZE THE RUBRIC

A rubric tells you what needs to be included in your writing.

Purpose, Focus, and Organization
Read the third bullet. What is a transitional strategy?

_____

_____

_____

_____

Evidence and Elaboration
Read the fifth bullet. What is the difference between academic and domain-specific language?

_____

_____

_____

Expository Writing Rubric

Purpose, Focus, and Organization • Score 4

- Stays focused on the purpose, audience, and task
- States the central idea in a clear way
- Uses transitional strategies, such as the use of signal, or linking, words and phrases, to show how ideas are connected
- Has a logical progression of ideas
- Begins with a strong introduction and ends with a conclusion

Evidence and Elaboration • Score 4

- Supports the central idea with convincing details
- Has strong examples of relevant evidence, or supporting details, with references to multiple sources
- Uses elaborative techniques, such as examples, definitions, and quotations from sources
- Uses precise language to express ideas clearly
- **Uses appropriate academic and domain-specific language that matches the audience and purpose of the essay**
- Uses different sentence types and lengths

Turn to page 236 for the complete Expository Writing Rubric.

Academic Language

Academic Vocabulary Academic language is the language of the classroom. It is often used in academic writing to communicate ideas. Academic language may be used in many different school subjects. Words such as *analyze, summarize, assess,* and *context* are examples of academic language. Read the paragraph below. An example of academic language is highlighted.

Purpose

Expository essays are written to share information, or to inform. Strong expository essays are supported by facts and carefully researched information.

> In addition, his version is longer than the original song. Some who have **analyzed** Hadfield's version say it begins at a slower tempo. He also altered some of the lyrics. His lyrics match his experiences with space travel. So, while the song is familiar to many listeners, Hadfield's version is unique.

How does the writer's use of academic language make it easier for the reader to understand the essay?

_____

_____

Central Idea Reread the paragraph. Underline the central idea of the paragraph. What examples of relevant evidence support it?

_____

ANALYZE THE STUDENT MODEL

Paragraph 1

Write a detail from Aliyah's introduction that caught your attention.

_____

_____

_____

Reread the first paragraph of Aliyah's essay. The central idea is highlighted.

Paragraphs 2–3

What is an example of relevant evidence that Aliyah uses to support the central idea in her introduction?

_____

_____

_____

Circle an example of domain-specific vocabulary.

Student Model: Expository Text

Aliyah responded to the writing prompt: _Write an expository essay about how an astronaut achieved his goal of bringing music to space._ Read Aliyah's essay below.

1   In 1961, Yuri Gagarin was the first astronaut sent to space. In 1969, Neil Armstrong was the first astronaut to walk on the moon. In 2013, an astronaut first recorded an album in space. This astronaut was Chris Hadfield. He is from Canada. He recorded it while on the International Space Station (ISS).

2   Space exploration has always involved trying out new things. Astronauts have learned how to move inside the capsules amid a lack of gravity. They have learned how to eat "space food." Animals have been sent into space. Cabbage and peas have been grown in space. But until 2013, no one had ever recorded a song in space as Hadfield did..

3   Hadfield is an astronaut and a musician. He has performed with bands. He has also performed live on TV. Hadfield recorded several songs while in space. But he also recorded a video. In the video, he recorded his version of a famous song. The song is called "Space Oddity." It is about an astronaut on a space mission.

4   But how exactly did Hadfield accomplish this? Let's summarize what he had to do. In the first source, "Music Man in Space," it says Hadfield needed to be careful. He had to be careful when he strummed his guitar. He also had to be careful when he moved. Moving too fast or too much could cause him to bump against computers and other equipment. The song is mostly a composition of his voice and his guitar.

5   In addition, his version is longer than the original song. Some who have analyzed Hadfield's version say it begins at a slower tempo. He also altered some of the lyrics. His lyrics match his experiences with space travel. So, while the song is familiar to many listeners, Hadfield's version is unique.

6   Hadfield made the video to show what it is like for humans in space. When he sings about how he is sitting "far above" Earth, the video shows him near a shuttle window with Earth in the distance. Many people felt this video added to the meaning of the song. Hadfield has said that he made his music video to let people see how humans have gone "beyond the planet" and "live in space." Clearly, his lyrics and his video allowed people to see exactly what he'd intended—the reality of a human living in space, far above the planet.

kali9/iStock/Getty Images Plus

EXPOSITORY ESSAY

Paragraph 4

Reread the fourth paragraph. **Underline** an example of academic language that Aliyah uses. How does the language help you understand the paragraph?

_____

_____

_____

Paragraphs 5-6

Underline an example of elaboration that Aliyah uses. What idea does this elaboration support?

_____

_____

_____

Apply the Rubric

With a partner, use the rubric on page 200 to discuss why Aliyah scored a 4 on her essay.

Analyze the Prompt

Writing Prompt

Write an expository essay to explain to your class why it is important to have different kinds of experts in space.

Purpose, Audience, and Task Reread the writing prompt. What is your purpose for writing? My purpose is to _____

_____

Who will your audience be? My audience will be _____

_____

What type of writing is the prompt asking for? _____

_____

Set a Purpose for Reading Sources Asking questions about why experts with different skills are needed on space missions will help you figure out your purpose for reading. It also helps you understand what you already know about the topic. Write a question below.

_____

_____

_____

Read the following passage set.

Astronauts Who Farm

1   Astronauts on the International Space Station (ISS) do many things. They analyze computer systems. They repair equipment, such as satellites. But did you know astronauts on the ISS also farm?

2   Scientists from around the world are achieving their goal to study how seeds and plants grow in space. In 2017, Joe Acaba and his crew members worked to grow vegetables they could eat. He harvested a type of green lettuce and a type of red lettuce. Peggy Whitson is an astronaut who has grown cabbage on the ISS. She once said she loves "gardening on Earth" and that gardening "is just as fun in space."

3   But not all astronauts know how to garden or farm. Sometimes they need a little help. So, there are scientists on Earth ready to help them out. Gioia Massa is one of those scientists. Massa talks to astronauts on the ISS about how to care for plants. She gives them tips. She and many others are working together to make sure these little space farms succeed.

This is an artist's idea of what it might be like to grow food on another planet. There are lights in the overhead bar. The lights are a combination of red, blue, and green to mimic the light the Sun gives off.

EXPOSITORY ESSAY

FIND TEXT EVIDENCE

Paragraph 1
Read paragraph 1. **Circle** an example of academic language.

Paragraph 2
Underline the elaborative techniques the author uses. What was the technique?

_____

Paragraph 3
Draw a box around the central idea of paragraph 3.

Picture and Caption
What do you learn from the picture and caption that you don't learn from the text?

_____

_____

_____

Take Notes Summarize the central idea of the source. Give examples of details that support it.

NASA

WRITING

FIND TEXT EVIDENCE

Paragraphs 4–5

Underline the central idea. Write an example of evidence that supports this idea.

_____

_____

Paragraphs 6–7

Write about how paragraphs 6 and 7 elaborate on the central idea in paragraph 4.

_____

_____

Paragraph 8

Write about how the conclusion ties back to the introduction.

_____

_____

_____

Take Notes Summarize the central idea of the source. Include details that support that idea.

Growing Vegetables in Space

4   For many years, scientists have wanted to understand if plants could be grown on other planets. Plants need water, nutrients, and sunlight to grow and thrive. These are bountiful on Earth. But these are not always available on other planets. For example, Mars has dust in its atmosphere that blocks sunlight. So, researchers have developed ways to grow plants in space.

5   The Advanced Plant Habitat (APH) is one invention. This is a unique system on board the International Space Station (ISS). Using the APH, the astronauts can control things like the amount of light and water plants get. Then the astronauts can take pictures and record the growth of plants. Scientists can use this information to better understand what plants need to thrive in space.

6   Another invention is the Veggie Passive Orbital Nutrient Delivery System. This is called PONDS for short. Seeds are placed into small PONDS units. Then these units are sent to the ISS. Each unit contains water and nutrients the seed needs to grow.

7   The Veggie Production System is another invention. It is a unit that can grow leafy greens. This invention is unique. The primary goal of this invention is providing fresh and healthy salads to astronauts on board the ISS.

8   Astronauts may be able to travel to other planets. If they do, they will need to grow much of their own food. These inventions will help humans live in space.

Spores in Space

9   Astronauts are growing plants in space. They have already grown flowers and vegetables. These are flowering plants. Flowering plants produce flowers and seeds. The seeds are how new plants are grown. But some students are working with astronauts to study mushrooms. They are fungi. They produce spores instead of seeds. A spore can grow into new fungi.

10   Students at Ryerson University wanted to know if a fungus, like a mushroom, could be grown on the International Space Station (ISS). There are many reasons to grow mushrooms in space. First of all, some types of mushrooms are healthy to eat, so they could be a good source of food for astronauts. Second of all, mushrooms can grow on many things. They do not necessarily need soil. They can be grown on leftover food scraps. As the mushrooms grow, they break down the leftovers. This means there would be less waste in space. Lastly, mushroom spores can survive harsh conditions. That makes spores ideal to transport into space.

11   The students worked with scientists. They put mushroom spores into a special tube. The tube was put on a rocket and launched to the ISS. According to NASA, the plan is for astronauts to try to grow these spores on the ISS. The hope is that the spores will grow into mushrooms. If they do, spores may be a way to feed astronauts in the future.

EXPOSITORY ESSAY

FIND TEXT EVIDENCE 🔍

Paragraph 9
Underline the central idea in paragraph 9. Write evidence that supports that idea.

_____

_____

Paragraph 10
Circle transitional strategies the writer uses in paragraph 10.

Paragraph 11
Draw a box around a source that is referenced. Why is it important to reference your sources in an essay?

_____

_____

_____

_____

📝 **Take Notes** Summarize the central idea of the source. Give examples of ideas that support it.

WRITING

My Goal I can synthesize information from three sources.

TAKE NOTES

Read the writing prompt below. Use the three sources, your notes, and the graphic organizer to plan a response.

Writing Prompt *Write an expository essay to present to your class about why experts with different skills are needed on space missions.*

Synthesize Information

Review the evidence recorded from each source. How does the information show how people who can grow plants are needed in space?

CHECK IN 1 2 3 4

Plan: Organize Ideas

Central Idea	Supporting Ideas
We need people with different skills, such as plant scientists, to become astronauts.	Plants grown in space can be used to feed astronauts.

Relevant Evidence		
Source 1	**Source 2**	**Source 3**
In 2017, Joe Acaba and his crew grew plants they could eat.		

Draft: Reference Sources

Paraphrase As you write your draft, remember to paraphrase, or use your own words to explain, the information from your sources that you recorded in your notes. When you use a source in your draft, remember to reference, or mention, it. Copying exact words from a source without saying where the words are from is called plagiarism. Read this sentence from Aliyah's essay.

> In the first source, "Music Man in Space," it says Hadfield needed to be careful.

Notice how Aliyah references the source. **Circle** the source. The title is in quotes. **Underline** the paraphrased idea Aliyah used in her essay.

Now reference one of the sources and paraphrase an idea you will use in your essay. Follow the model above.

_____

_____

_____

Draft Use your graphic organizer and example above to write your draft in your writer's notebook. Before you start writing, review the rubric on page 200. Remember to reference your sources.

Quick Tip

When you paraphrase, remember to avoid copying from your source. To paraphrase, look away from your source when taking notes. Jot down relevant details in your own words. Then check your notes against the original source.

CHECK IN 1 2 3 4

Revise: Peer Conferences

Review a Draft Listen actively to your partner. Take notes about what you liked and what was difficult to follow. Begin by telling what you liked. Use these sentence starters.

I like the evidence you used to support the central idea because . . .

What did you mean by . . .

I think adding references to your sources helps to . . .

After you finish giving each other feedback, reflect on the peer conference. What suggestion did you find to be the most helpful?

_____

_____

Revision Use the Revising Checklist to figure out what text you may need to move, elaborate on, or delete. After you finish your final draft, use the full rubric on pages 236–239 to score your essay.

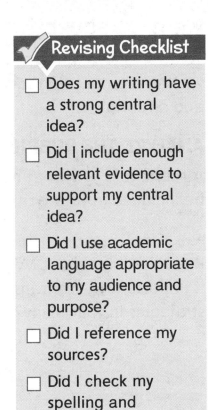

Revising Checklist

☐ Does my writing have a strong central idea?

☐ Did I include enough relevant evidence to support my central idea?

☐ Did I use academic language appropriate to my audience and purpose?

☐ Did I reference my sources?

☐ Did I check my spelling and punctuation?

Next, you'll write an expository essay on a new topic.

My Score			
Purpose, Focus, & Organization (4 pts)	Evidence & Elaboration (4 pts)	Conventions (2 pts)	Total (10 pts)

WRITE TO SOURCES

You will answer an expository writing prompt using sources and a rubric.

ANALYZE THE RUBRIC

A rubric tells you what needs to be included in your writing.

Purpose, Focus, and Organization

Read the third bullet. Why is it important to use transitional strategies in your essay?

_____

_____

_____

Evidence and Elaboration

Read the third bullet. What are elaborative techniques?

_____

_____

Is the word *summarize* an example of academic or domain-specific language?

_____

Expository Writing Rubric

Purpose, Focus, and Organization • Score 4

- Stays focused on the purpose, audience, and task
- States the central idea in a clear way
- Uses transitional strategies, such as the use of signal, or linking, words and phrases, to show how ideas are connected
- Has a logical progression of ideas
- Begins with a strong introduction and ends with a conclusion

Evidence and Elaboration • Score 4

- Supports the central idea with convincing details
- Has strong examples of relevant evidence, or supporting details, with references to multiple sources
- **Uses elaborative techniques, such as examples, definitions, and quotations from sources**
- Uses precise language to express ideas clearly
- Uses appropriate academic and domain-specific language that matches the audience and purpose of the essay
- Uses different sentence types and lengths

Turn to page 236 for the complete Expository Writing Rubric.

Valentain Jevee/Shutterstock

Relevant Evidence

Audience

Keep your audience in mind when you write your essay. You should use a formal tone when writing an expository essay. You would use a friendly tone if you were writing a letter to a classmate.

Elaborative Techniques Relevant evidence is the set of facts you include in your essay that support your central idea. Strong expository essays use elaborative techniques, such as definitions, examples, and quotes, to further explain your evidence. These add depth and interest to the essay, while adding more support to the central idea. Read the paragraph below. The elaborative technique is highlighted.

> There's a lot of research on this issue. **The *New York Times* states that "the average person spends 90 percent of his or her time indoors."** Being indoors too much can be bad for a person's health.

How does the quote help develop the idea that being indoors too much can be bad for a person's health?

_____

_____

Definitions One way to elaborate on an idea is to include definitions in your essay. You can define a term right in the same sentence. Just separate the term and its definition with a comma and the word *or*. For example: *There's a lot of research, or study, on this issue.* Add a definition for the word *polluted* in the following sentence: *Indoor air can be polluted.*

_____

WRITING

ANALYZE THE STUDENT MODEL

Paragraph 1

Write a detail from Alvaro's introduction that caught your attention.

_____

_____

_____

Paragraph 2

Underline the central idea in paragraph 2.

Reread the second paragraph of Alvaro's essay. An example of elaboration is highlighted.

How does the elaboration develop the central idea?

_____

_____

_____

Alvaro responded to the writing prompt: *How does outdoor activity improve your health?* Read Alvaro's essay below.

1   Every day, I see kids at school get into trouble. Some kids have problems sitting still or following the teacher's directions. Other kids pick fights, or they exclude people. Some kids don't get into trouble. But it's clear that they are frustrated or stressed. There is something our schools can do to help. Schools can get kids outdoors and moving! Outdoor physical activity has been shown to help with all these problems.

2   There's a lot of research on this issue. The *New York Times* states that "the average person spends 90 percent of his or her time indoors." Being indoors too much can be bad for a person's health. Indoor air can be polluted. For example, it might contain mold or pollen. Indoor air, even in the cleanest places, can contain dust. Paint that is wearing off walls can release dangerous chemicals into the air. The air quality in schools may be particularly bad. The United States Occupational Safety and Health Administration (OSHA) states that many school buildings are old and in "poor condition." That means that these old schools are more likely to have air pollution.

3   This research means everyone needs to be outside and active a whole lot more. This is particularly true for students. Being active can help kids focus. Some physical activities, like yoga, have even been shown to help kids' moods. Active kids might feel less stressed.

4   Schools may find it hard to get kids outside. A lot of schools have kids spend most of their days in the classroom. The hope is that more time in the classroom means these students will learn better and succeed. But time outside on the playground is just as important. Kids will be better in the classroom if they have more outdoor activity.

5   Peaceful Playgrounds is a group that offers free posters to schools. The posters give ideas for being active outside. Schools can hang the posters in hallways. These reminders might help students and staff remember to get outside! Also, the LiiNK project is helping schools. They found that giving students short breaks to play outside made a difference. Students were more "focused in the classroom." Their "fidgeting decreased." And misbehavior "significantly decreased."

6   Time outdoors can solve many problems for students. There are many things schools can do to make outdoor activity part of student life. Let's get moving!

Russ Rohde/Cultura RF/Image Source

Paragraph 3

Write an example of elaboration that Alvaro used to further develop his central idea.

_____

_____

Paragraphs 4–5

Circle a signal, or linking, word in paragraph 4. How does the word link two ideas?

_____

_____

_____

_____

Paragraph 6

Draw a box around ideas from the introduction that are restated in the conclusion.

Apply the Rubric

With a partner, use the rubric on page 212 to discuss why Alvaro scored a 4 on his essay.

My Goal

I can write an expository essay.

Analyze the Prompt

Writing Prompt

Write an expository essay to explain to your class why play is an important activity.

Purpose, Audience, and Task Reread the writing prompt. What is your purpose for writing? My purpose is to _____

_____

Who will your audience be? My audience will be _____

_____

What type of writing is the prompt asking for? _____

_____

Set a Purpose for Reading Sources Asking questions about why play is an important activity will help you figure out your purpose for reading. It also helps you understand what you already know about the topic. Before you read the passage set about why play is an important activity, write a question on the lines below.

_____

_____

Why Do Animals Play?

1   Why do animals play? For the same reason YOU play—because it's FUN! **But for animals in the wild, play is important to their survival.**

2   A young deer will leap and frolic. It is learning how to run fast and zigzag to confuse predators. While deer have to learn to escape from predators, lion cubs must learn how to hunt. When a cub is little, it stalks its brother or sister. The cub pounces! The cubs keep their claws in, though, and their bites are gentle. This is practice for the real thing.

3   Much like human children, young dolphins love to explore their world. A piece of seaweed might inspire a game. Frisky calves chase one another, passing the seaweed from snout, to flipper, to tail.

4   When young animals wrestle, race, or chase, they are building strength and skills. And they are learning to cooperate. **If one youngster plays too rough, the others will let him know they are unhappy with his behavior.**

5   Young mountain goats live on steep slopes. If they're not careful, kids, or young goats, can fall and hurt their legs. When they play, the young animals learn to keep their footing. Just like you, animals have to learn about dangers in their world. Playing helps them learn. Playing makes them strong and confident.

EXPOSITORY ESSAY

FIND TEXT EVIDENCE

Paragraphs 1–2
Read the highlighted central idea in paragraph 1. **Draw a box around** the details in paragraph 2 that support the central idea.

Paragraph 3
Underline one way that play is important to animals. Summarize it on the line below.

_____

Paragraphs 4-5
Read the highlighted detail in paragraph 4. How does it support the central idea of the paragraph?

_____

_____

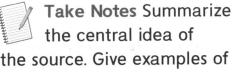 **Take Notes** Summarize the central idea of the source. Give examples of details that support it.

Paragraph 6

Underline the central idea.

Circle the signal words and phrases. How do they help you understand what you will read?

_____

_____

Paragraphs 7–9

Describe how the essay provides examples to elaborate on and support the central idea.

_____

_____

Photograph

What do you learn from the photograph?

_____

_____

Take Notes Summarize the central idea. Give details that support that idea.

SOURCE 2

Playgrounds GROW UP

6   Long ago, people did not believe that it was important for children to play. Over time, this view changed.

7   In 1885, Boston opened a sand garden for young children. This playground was a sand pile in an empty lot. But city children loved having a safe place to play.

8   Early playgrounds were designed to build strong bodies. Then, some people thought that playing together would help children become good citizens. Later, people saw that play helps children learn. As a result, schools added playgrounds. In New York City, there were dozens of playgrounds by the early 1900s.

9   By the 1970s, playgrounds mostly looked the same. They usually had monkey bars, swings, and so on. But some designers started building more creative play spaces. Instead of big equipment, many new playgrounds feature loose parts and open spaces. Now, kids can exercise their imaginations as much as their bodies.

Learning from Laughing RATS

10   The man tickled the rat in the glass box. He took notes. Why? The man is an animal behavior scientist. His research shows that animals are more like us than we knew. Rats enjoy being tickled. It makes them laugh.

11   Rats don't really giggle. A tickled rat makes a high-pitched sound that we can't hear without special equipment. Scientists think this sound is rat laughter.

12   Scientists have observed many kinds of animals playing and laughing. For example, chimpanzees and gorillas sometimes make sounds like laughter when they are tickled or when they are pretending to fight. The laughing sounds may signal that the animals are playing. Otherwise, a play fight might turn into a real one!

13   People laugh for many reasons. Laughter makes us feel good. It helps us relax. We laugh most when we are with others. Laughing together helps us get along better.

14   Scientists don't know all the reasons why animals play and laugh. However, the more we study animals at play, the more we may learn about ourselves.

Like humans, animals seem to enjoy doing things just for fun.

Jagodka/Shutterstock

EXPOSITORY ESSAY

FIND TEXT EVIDENCE

Paragraph 10
Underline the central idea in paragraph 10. **Draw a box around** the evidence that supports the central idea.

Paragraphs 11–12
Explain how the essay provides examples to elaborate on and support the central idea.

_____

_____

Paragraphs 13–14
Circle the signal phrase in paragraph 13. How does the phrase help you understand the ideas in the paragraph?

_____

_____

_____

Take Notes Summarize the central idea and give details that support it.

WRITING

My Goal I can synthesize information from three sources.

TAKE NOTES

Read the writing prompt below. Use the three sources, your notes, and the graphic organizer to plan your essay.

Writing Prompt *Write an expository essay explaining why play is an important activity.*

Synthesize Information

Think about what you know about playing. How do details from the sources and your own knowledge about playing help you support the central idea? Discuss your ideas with a partner.

Plan: Organize Ideas

Introduction State the central idea.	Playing is an important activity.

Body Supporting Ideas	Playing helps people get along.

Conclusion Restate the central idea.	

CHECK IN ⟩ 1 ⟩ 2 ⟩ 3 ⟩ 4

Relevant Evidence		
Source 1	Source 2	Source 3
As with humans, when animals play, it teaches them to cooperate.		

Valentain Jevee/Shutterstock

Draft: Transitional Strategies

Connecting Ideas Transitional strategies, such as using signal, or linking, words and phrases, help to connect ideas in an essay. The signal words *and, also*, and *another* can show ideas are related. The words *but* and *however* can show how ideas are different. The phrases *such as, for example*, and *for instance* can show an example of an idea. Using signal words can clarify your ideas.

Read the sentences below.

> They explore their world. A piece of seaweed might inspire a game.

Rewrite the above sentences. Use signal words or phrases to connect the two ideas.

_____

_____

_____

Draft Use your graphic organizer and the example above to write your draft in your writer's notebook. Before you start writing, review the rubric on page 212. Remember to indent each paragraph.

Grammar Connections

When writing about an animal in general, use the pronoun *it*, not *him* or *her*. And remember, a possessive pronoun does not have an apostrophe because no letters are missing. So *its long tail* is correct; *it's long tail* is not correct.

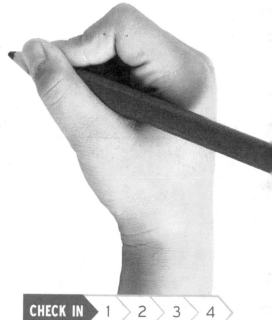

CHECK IN 1 2 3 4

Revise: Peer Conferences

Review a Draft Listen actively to your partner. Take notes about what you liked and what was difficult to follow. Begin by telling what you liked. Use these sentence starters.

I like the evidence you used to support the central idea because . . .

What did you mean by . . .

I think adding signal words helps to . . .

After you finish giving each other feedback, reflect on the peer conference. What suggestion did you find to be the most helpful?

_____

_____

Revision Use the Revising Checklist to figure out what text you may need to move, elaborate on, or delete. After you finish your final draft, use the full rubric on pages 236 to 239 to score your essay.

Turn to page 199. Fill in the bars to show what you learned.

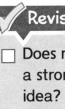

✓ Revising Checklist

☐ Does my writing have a strong central idea?

☐ Did I include enough relevant evidence to support my central idea?

☐ Did I use good linking words to show the connections among ideas?

☐ Do I have a strong introduction?

☐ Did I check my spelling and punctuation?

My Score			
Purpose, Focus, & Organization (4 pts)	Evidence & Elaboration (4 pts)	Conventions (2 pts)	Total (10 pts)

My Goal I can read and understand social studies texts.

TAKE NOTES

Take notes and annotate as you read the passages "Why Dog's Nose Is Cold" and "All About Folktales."

Look for the answer to the question. *How do stories help us understand the world around us?*

_____

_____

_____

_____

_____

_____

_____

PASSAGE 1   CARIBBEAN FOLKTALE

Why Dog's Nose Is Cold

Long ago in the islands of the Caribbean, there was a great storm. The storm wiped out the honey bees, so there was no honey. The storm destroyed the fruit on the trees. There were no mangos, no bananas, not even a tart tamarind to eat.

Man walked alone in the jungles. Man was very hungry. This is when he first began to hunt animals. He aimed his bow and arrow at Wild Pig. He let his arrow fly and missed! The man tried again. He let an arrow fly at Woodpecker. He missed! Again, the man took aim at Parrot. Again, he missed!

Man walked out of the jungle as hungry as can be. And the animals were no longer his friends. Word went around the jungle. "Man is a hunter! Keep out of his way!" The animals now all warned each other when Man entered the jungle. The birds sang the warning every time Man approached and tried to enter the forest.

Now, Man was alone. No animal showed him friendship. He went to the jungle, and all eyes were on him. It was the cold eyes of Snake, the fierce red eyes of Baboon, the burning yellow eyes of Jaguar. He knew these were not the eyes of friends, but the eyes of hunters like himself.

Man knew he could no longer go into the jungle alone. Man went to the river to catch fish. That was the only food for him.

The Sun spirit Arawidi saw that Man was catching all the fish. This was not good. He decided to give Man an animal as a friend. That evening, Man laid out the fish he had caught of all sizes and colors. Arawidi appeared. He took a fish in each of his hands and shaped them into the body of a dog. He gave it legs. He shaped the head of a fish into the head of a dog. The part of the head that Arawidi held in his hands became the nose, but it remained cold like a fish.

So it is that there is a dog in every Carib's house, watching over him at night, helping him hunt during the day. And so it is that every dog has a cold nose.

TAKE NOTES

TAKE NOTES

_____

_____

_____

_____

_____

_____

_____

_____

_____

_____

_____

_____

_____

PASSAGE 2

EXPOSITORY TEXT

All About Folktales

Long before people could write, they told stories. Storytellers passed down these folktales from one generation to the next. People retold the tales in different ways. Today, we can read many versions of the same story.

Folktales had several purposes. Some explained natural events that people didn't understand. Many taught a lesson about life, called a moral. Most importantly, all folktales entertained their listeners. Some stories described amazing places or scary monsters. In others, the characters, like the spider Anansi, played tricks on each other.

There is always a problem in a folktale, but the characters find a way to solve it. These characters can be ordinary people, such as farmers. They can even be animals, like the shy Turtle, who speak and act just like people.

Folktales teach us about the ancient beliefs and customs of different cultures. They come from all over the world, including North and South America, the Caribbean, Asia, and Africa. When we read these stories, we connect with these cultures in a special way.

COMPARE THE PASSAGES

Review your notes on "All About Folktales" and "Why Dog's Nose Is Cold." Then create a Venn diagram. Use your notes and the diagram to compare how what you learned in the passages is alike and different.

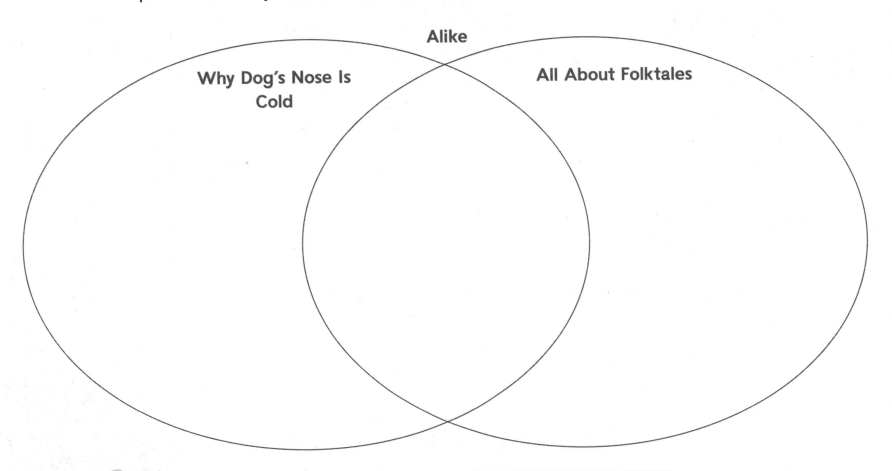

Alike

Why Dog's Nose Is Cold

All About Folktales

Synthesize Information

How does "All About Folktales" help you better understand "Why Dog's Nose Is Cold"? What does "Why Dog's Nose Is Cold" teach you about the world around you?

CHECK IN 1 ⟩ 2 ⟩ 3 ⟩ 4

PLAN YOUR OWN ANIMAL TALE

You've read many tales about animals. Now let's write your own!

Main Character: Think about who your main character will be. Write three interesting traits, or things that are special about the character. Draw an illustration to show what your main character looks like.

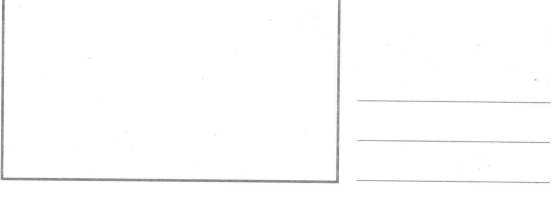

Other Characters: Who are the other characters in your tale? Will they get along with your main character, or will there be conflict?

Your Message: What message do you want to share in your tale? Will you explain something in nature? Will you teach a lesson?

Setting: Where will your tale take place? Describe the setting.

WRITE YOUR OWN ANIMAL TALE

Complete the outline below. Use your outline to write your tale.

Beginning: How will your tale begin? How will you introduce your characters? What event could grab your reader's attention?

_____

_____

Middle: What will be the conflict in your tale? Will the characters need to solve a problem? Is there a disagreement between characters? Is there a question that needs to be answered?

_____

_____

_____

Ending: How will your characters solve their problem or answer their question? How can you share your message so readers understand?

_____

_____

Share your outline with a partner. Describe your characters and what will happen in your tale. Then use your plan and outline to write your tale. Remember to give it a title. You can also add illustrations.

My Goal I can read and understand science texts.

TAKE NOTES

Take notes and annotate as you read the passages "Watching the Stars: The Story of Maria Mitchell" and "Exoplanets Are Out of This World!"

Look for the answer to the question. *How does observing the world around us lead to important discoveries?*

_____

_____

_____

_____

_____

PASSAGE **1**
EXPOSITORY TEXT

Watching the Stars: The Story of Maria Mitchell

A small streak in the sky might not seem like much, but on October 1, 1847, Maria Mitchell recognized that blurry streak in her telescope as a brand-new comet. Mitchell was unknown at the time, and she might have stayed unknown. There were no recognized female astronomers. Many leading scientists might have ignored her contributions, but today, she is recognized as the first female astronomer. How was she able to overcome such a huge obstacle? She worked hard and had an important supporter— her father.

Maria Mitchell was born on August 1, 1818. Her love of astronomy started in her childhood. Mitchell's father was a teacher and an astronomer. He made sure that all his children received the same education. This was unusual at the time. Most families only educated boys. Mitchell's father taught her how to use their family's telescope. She studied hard and followed in his footsteps. She spent every clear night she could observing the night sky.

Science History Images/Alamy Stock Photo

After Mitchell graduated, she worked as a librarian for twenty years. She worked all day among books, and then she spent her evenings among the stars. On that night in October 1847, Mitchell noted her discovery and ran to tell her father. He announced the news of her discovery to the scientific community.

Mitchell's discovery made her famous around the world. She became the first woman to be elected to the American Academy of Arts and Sciences. She toured the world and met scientists. Many women's groups celebrated her success. In 1865, she became a professor at Vassar Female College. She was the first female professor of astronomy in the country. She was also a pioneer in the study of sunspots.

Mitchell was an inspiration to her students. They often asked, "Did you learn that from a book, or did you observe it yourself?" She led her students in direct observations of solar eclipses.

Maria Mitchell died in 1889, but her legacy is celebrated even today. Her research and observations brought us all a little closer to the stars.

Interim Archives/Archive Photos/Getty Images

CONNECT TO CONTENT

TAKE NOTES

_____

_____

_____

_____

_____

_____

_____

_____

_____

_____

_____

_____

_____

_____

EXPOSITORY TEXT

Exoplanets Are OUᵗ of This World!

An exoplanet is a planet that is not part of the solar system and does not orbit the Sun. Instead, it orbits stars outside the solar system. Exoplanets are difficult to detect. They cannot be easily found using typical telescopes, so for many years, researchers thought that exoplanets were rare. But now researchers know that they are actually very common.

Researchers developed special tools and methods to detect exoplanets. As of 2018, there have been over 3,900 exoplanets discovered. One of the most remarkable exoplanets is known as WASP-142b. What makes this planet special is that it was discovered by a fifteen-year-old student. Tom Wagg was a space buff. He had the chance to work in a special university program and found the exoplanet when reviewing data. The planet he discovered is over 1,000 light years away!

Cameras like this one are around the world, searching for any detection of exoplanets.

Enrico Sacchetti/Science Source

COMPARE THE PASSAGES

Review your notes on "Watching the Stars: The Story of Maria Mitchell" and "Exoplanets Are Out of This World!" Create a Venn diagram like the one below. Use your notes and the diagram to compare how what you learned in the passages is alike and different.

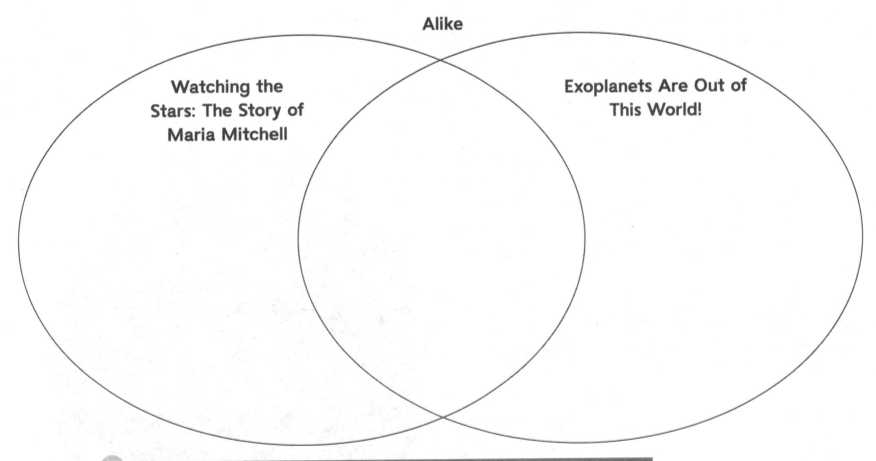

Alike

Watching the Stars: The Story of Maria Mitchell

Exoplanets Are Out of This World!

🔍 **Synthesize Information**

Think about both texts. How has observation of the sky helped us learn more about space? Why is observation important to science?

CHECK IN   1   2   3   4

SCIENCE

CREATE YOUR OWN CONSTELLATION

A group of stars is called a constellation. People all over the world and throughout time have looked up at the stars. They've seen patterns in the stars and created pictures and stories to go with those patterns. What patterns do you see in the night sky?

With an adult, go out at night and gaze up at the stars. Look for a pattern, or shape. Do you see an animal? A person? Something from nature? Draw what you see on a piece of paper.

Many constellations have stories to explain them. Write a story to explain your constellation. How did it find its place among the stars?

If you can't find a pattern you like, you can use Ursa Major, or the Great Bear. It is made up of one of the easiest constellations to observe, the Big Dipper. Create a story that explains how the Great Bear became part of the night sky.

Share your constellation story with a partner. You can also read it or act it out for your class.

The Big Dipper is outlined in red in the image. A dipper is like a big spoon that people would dip into a bucket or well so they could get a drink of water.

amana images inc./Alamy Stock Photo

Reflect on Your Learning

Talk About It Reflect on what you learned in this unit. Then talk with a partner about how you did.

I am really proud of how I can _____

_____

_____

_____

Something I need to work more on is _____

_____

_____

_____

My Goal Set a goal for the next grade. In your reader's notebook, write about what you can do to get there.

Share a goal you have with a partner.

Expository Writing Rubric

Score	Purpose, Focus, and Organization (4-point Rubric)	Evidence and Elaboration (4-point Rubric)	Conventions of Standard English (2-point Rubric)
4	• Stays focused on the purpose, audience, and task • States the central idea in a clear way • Uses transitional strategies, such as the use of signal, or linking, words and phrases, to show how ideas are connected • Has a logical progression of ideas • Begins with a strong introduction and ends with a conclusion	• Supports the central idea with convincing details • Has strong examples of relevant evidence, or supporting details, with references to multiple sources • Uses elaborative techniques, such as examples, definitions, and quotations from sources • Uses precise language to express ideas clearly • Uses appropriate academic and domain-specific language that matches the audience and purpose of the essay • Uses different sentence types and lengths	

Score	Purpose, Focus, and Organization (4-point Rubric)	Evidence and Elaboration (4-point Rubric)	Conventions of Standard English (2-point Rubric)
3	• Stays mostly focused on the purpose, audience, and task • States the central idea in a mostly clear way • Uses some transitional strategies, such as the use of signal, or linking, words and phrases, to show how ideas are connected • Has a mostly logical progression of ideas • Begins with an introduction and ends with a conclusion	• Supports the central idea with mostly convincing details • Has examples of relevant evidence, or supporting details, with references to multiple sources • Uses some elaborative techniques, such as examples, definitions, and quotations from sources • Uses some precise language to express ideas clearly • Uses some appropriate academic and domain-specific language that matches the audience and purpose of the essay • Uses some different sentence types and lengths	

Expository Writing Rubric

Score	Purpose, Focus, and Organization (4-point Rubric)	Evidence and Elaboration (4-point Rubric)	Conventions of Standard English (2-point Rubric)
2	• Stays somewhat focused on the purpose, audience, and task • States the central idea, but sometimes the central idea isn't clear • Uses a few transitional strategies, such as the use of signal, or linking, words and phrases, to show how ideas are connected • Has an uneven progression of ideas • Has an unsatisfactory introduction or conclusion	• Gives some very basic support of the central idea • Has unsatisfactory examples of evidence, or supporting details, with few references to multiple sources • Uses a few weak elaborative techniques • Uses imprecise or simple expression of ideas • Uses inappropriate or unsatisfactory academic and domain-specific language • Uses only simple sentences	• Shows a satisfactory understanding of grammar and spelling • Includes small errors, but no patterns of errors • Use of punctuation, capitalization, sentence structure, and spelling is satisfactory

Score	Purpose, Focus, and Organization (4-point Rubric)	Evidence and Elaboration (4-point Rubric)	Conventions of Standard English (2-point Rubric)
1	• Shows some relationship to the topic but shows little awareness of the purpose, audience, and task • Has little or no central idea • Has little or no organization • Has confusing or unclear ideas • Uses a few or no transitional strategies • Has many unrelated ideas that make the essay difficult to understand • Shows little understanding of the topic	• Gives very little support of the central idea • Has little, if any, use of sources, facts, and details • Has very little or no examples of evidence from the sources • Has little or no relevant or accurate evidence • Uses an expression of ideas that is not clear or is confusing • Inappropriate or unsatisfactory academic and domain-specific language • Uses only simple sentences	• Shows a partial understanding of grammar and spelling • Includes many errors in usage • Has an unsatisfactory use of punctuation, capitalization, sentence structure, and spelling
0			• Shows a lack of understanding of grammar and spelling • Includes serious errors, making the essay difficult to understand

Opinion Writing Rubric

Score	Purpose, Focus, and Organization (4-point Rubric)	Evidence and Elaboration (4-point Rubric)	Conventions of Standard English (2-point Rubric)
4	• Stays focused on the purpose, audience, and task • States the opinion in a clear way • Uses transitional strategies, such as the use of signal, or linking, words and phrases, to show how ideas are connected • Has a logical progression of ideas • Begins with a strong introduction and ends with a conclusion	• Supports the opinion with convincing details • Has strong examples of relevant evidence, or supporting details, with references to multiple sources • Uses elaborative techniques, such as examples, definitions, and quotations from sources • Uses precise language to express ideas clearly • Uses appropriate academic and domain-specific language that matches the audience and purpose of the essay • Uses different sentence types and lengths	

Score	Purpose, Focus, and Organization (4-point Rubric)	Evidence and Elaboration (4-point Rubric)	Conventions of Standard English (2-point Rubric)
3	• Stays mostly focused on the purpose, audience, and task • States the opinion in a mostly clear way • Uses some transitional strategies, such as the use of signal, or linking, words and phrases, to show how ideas are connected • Has a mostly logical progression of ideas • Begins with an introduction and ends with a conclusion	• Supports the opinion with mostly convincing details • Has examples of relevant evidence, or supporting details, with references to multiple sources • Uses some elaborative techniques, such as examples, definitions, and quotations from sources • Uses some precise language to express ideas clearly • Uses some appropriate academic and domain-specific language that matches the audience and purpose of the essay • Uses some different sentence types and lengths	

Opinion Writing Rubric

Score	Purpose, Focus, and Organization (4-point Rubric)	Evidence and Elaboration (4-point Rubric)	Conventions of Standard English (2-point Rubric)
2	• Stays somewhat focused on the purpose, audience, and task • States the opinion, but sometimes the opinion isn't clear • Uses a few transitional strategies, such as the use of signal, or linking, words and phrases, to show how ideas are connected • Has an uneven progression of ideas • Has an unsatisfactory introduction or conclusion	• Gives some very basic support of the opinion • Has unsatisfactory examples of evidence, or supporting details, with few references to multiple sources • Uses a few weak elaborative techniques • Uses imprecise or simple expression of ideas • Uses inappropriate or unsatisfactory academic and domain-specific language • Uses only simple sentences	• Shows a satisfactory understanding of grammar and spelling • Includes small errors, but no patterns of errors • Use of punctuation, capitalization, sentence structure, and spelling is satisfactory

Score	Purpose, Focus, and Organization (4-point Rubric)	Evidence and Elaboration (4-point Rubric)	Conventions of Standard English (2-point Rubric)
1	• Shows some relationship to the topic but shows little awareness of the purpose, audience, and task • Has little or no opinion • Has little or no organization • Has confusing or unclear ideas • Uses a few or no transitional strategies • Has many unrelated ideas that make the essay difficult to understand • Shows little understanding of the topic	• Gives very little support of the opinion • Has little, if any, use of sources, facts, and details • Has very little or no examples of evidence from the sources • Has little or no relevant or accurate evidence • Uses an expression of ideas that is not clear or is confusing • Includes inappropriate or unsatisfactory academic and domain-specific language • Uses only simple sentences	• Shows a partial understanding of grammar and spelling • Includes many errors in usage • Has an unsatisfactory use of punctuation, capitalization, sentence structure, and spelling
0			• Shows a lack of understanding of grammar and spelling • Includes serious errors, making the essay difficult to understand